25265.

D0257885

TELEPEN

THE IMAGERY OF POWER

The Imagery of Power

A Critique of Advertising

by

FRED INGLIS

HEINEMANN · LONDON

Heinemann Educational Books Ltd
LONDON EDINBURGH MELBOURNE
SINGAPORE JOHANNESBURG
IBADAN HONG KONG NEW DELHI
TORONTO AUCKLAND
KUALA LUMPUR NAIROBI

ISBN 0 435 18470 9

Published by
Heinemann Educational Books Ltd
48 Charles Street, London W1X 8AH
Made and printed in Great Britain by
William Clowes & Sons, Limited
London, Beccles and Colchester

Contents

List of Plates

For Raymond Williams

Author's Note

As I say in its pages, this book follows in the line of dissent marked out by the critics of modern industrial civilization. More particularly, I have tried to develop the arguments against advertising which begin with *Culture and Environment* and are taken up in Denys Thompson's *Voice of Civilization*. But I also owe to Denys Thompson an enormous amount of information quarried from many sources and supplied for my use in this book. His presence in it, therefore, is far more immediate than as a voice from the past. He made the book possible in a historic sense, by creating a systematic language of criticism for mass communications; he also made it possible by hard and tedious work in libraries and at home, and by promptly and generously supplying any information I asked for. Similarly, Frank Whitehead, himself a pioneer of such criticism, supplied boxes of cuttings and examples for me to sift and use, and Michael Barratt Brown, another lifelong member of that small group of social radicals who have kept alive the voice of dissent, most generously loaned me an unpublished paper which forms the basis for large parts of the general economic critique in Chapter Two. His remarkably prescient paper was written over ten years ago, and he may consequently not agree now with my extensive reformulations of what he said. But I couldn't have managed without the gift of his insights and thought. Lastly, I want to pay unaffected tribute to Raymond Williams, whose books and journalism as well as whose personal warmth and unchecked kindness, the strength of his participation in day-to-day political life, provide an occasion for natural admiration and loyalty at a time when intellectual life is so often trivial or dishonest.

Foreword

When Fred Inglis undertook to revise a book of mine on advertising (*Voice of Civilisation*, 1944) he found that a mere bringing up to date was out of the question. A new climate of opinion, owing much to developments in sociology and psychology; changes in advertising itself; a scepticism about economic 'growth'—these necessitated a different aim, approach and method, and have resulted in a fresh, wider-ranging, and much better book.

The contempt commonly expressed for advertising nowadays and the boredom produced by the adman's bromides about 'freedom of choice' boil down to little more than dissatisfaction with a remediable excrescence. But that is just what advertising is not; and the apologies made for it conceal its *raison d'être*. It is in fact an integral part of an economic set-up that is not only inefficient at husbanding and using the resources at its disposal, but even when it works—when there is 'growth' and full employment—is incompetent to provide a human way of living and an objective that commands respect. Fred Inglis shows how advertising is locked firmly into the communications system that is mobilized by our economics, and offers a succinct analysis of that system, exposing the true worth of the abundance it offers and the extent to which real scarcity is ignored by the mass consumer market. In so doing he throws light on much else and uncovers the connections between a number of activities that appear to be separate.

Advertising is essential to our economic system, because it disguises the truth and encourages forms of behaviour that maintain the system and make it seem tolerable. Advertising ensures a conforming population of consumers through its control of Press and TV, which filter the information that reaches us, decide for many of us our view of social reality, and safely canalize even the apparent dissidence of the pop scene. Its ethics—and this is one of the most impressive insights of the book—powerfully suffuse the whole system of communication. As the theology of the status quo it aims at controlling our lives and keeping us on the consumer treadmill.

Finally, three quotations. Advertising 'is a main voice in our culture and what it says is very largely malignant'. 'Every advertisement we see implicitly derides the culture, the physical uprightness, the dignity and social justice which make a living civilization possible.' 'The study (of advertising) should help enlarge that area where we call ourselves our own men.' Thus the subject of this book is radically hostile to education, and becomes the business of everyone concerned for education—this much is generally recognized. It does not mean that much time in school should be devoted to criticism of advertising; not every new adult preoccupation can squeeze into the curriculum. But a start should be given, and in a context of effective education—which really is to be found in a number of schools—it is the start that matters. The nature and extent of work on advertising are matters for teachers, and it is they who need the clearest understanding of society, so that with aims defined they can make rational selection from the great field of material that lies around them. All who seek this understanding will find Fred Inglis's book invaluable; radical, incisive, lively in every line, it stands alone in its field and is unlikely to be superseded for many years.

DENYS THOMPSON

ONE

The Genetics of Advertising

Advertising is a process of a particular society. It cannot be liberated from that society if we want to understand its meanings, and it is symptomatic that a discussion of advertising such as this book intends has to start with such a commonplace. In our peculiarly English innocence, we discuss advertisements—whether admiringly or with derision—in such a way as almost to empty them of sponsorship. Of course people say, 'You can't believe the adman' or 'They are only trying to con you'; at more technical levels, in the textbooks of secondary or higher education, one may find a sharp distaste for the commercial implications of mass advertising and the moral implications of mass persuasion. But one does not find an adequate theory of mass communication and of the social relations which subsume and generate communication. The scrutiny of advertising requires that we lodge it securely within a sponsoring structure and we mark out the main features of that structure. We should not discuss the process and the activity of advertising by itself. The linguistic and intellectual boundaries of the last two hundred years have taught us that a necessary antecedent of inquiry is to isolate the phenomenon in order to look at it hard enough. The scientific ethic of the nineteenth century which still dominates the social sciences works to cut off effect from cause and to prevent our making the essential connections between human activities. A conventional hard-headedness in our culture demands that we provide as the results of a critical inquiry information which will answer the bald questions, 'What are its laws? What are its co-ordinates? Its mass, form and relations?' But hard-headedness at a quite early stage becomes philistinism. There are certain kinds of formal knowledge which will be denied us if we insist on knowing as only being possible in this technical sense. What is needed is for us to be able to construct terms of reference with which to analyse and understand the mass communications of our time, and advertising as a style of such communication which interpenetrates and suffuses all forms.

The major creative effort by the artists and writers of this century has been to diagnose and give expression to the experience of industrial and urban living. The disunity and solitude of so much of our lives have come to seem necessary conditions rather than the product of particular forces manipulated not by the force of destiny or technology, but by groups of men in conflict with other men. The idea of disjuncture—the gap between our lives and our society, especially our lives and our work—is present as an image in our every day language. The sociological charts and the real language of men corroborate each other's bearings. They speak of a man losing all sense of community and common purpose, divided in himself between some notion of his true being and a homogenized, sociable version of that being dictated to him by his social structure. In so many ways, even in a fairly placid society like Britain's, small social actions— unofficial strikes, minor demonstrations, letters to the local paper, refusals to pay rates or to move out of condemned property—these actions take the moral measure of the power of society over the individual, and of those diminishing and already tiny areas where a man can call himself his own. The loss of connection, the retreat into silence, the slow, visible decay of friends or near relations beneath the heavy pressures of work and the social experience of our society, all this we have seen, nearby and at home. This much is incontrovertible. We have felt the terrible weight of society-out-there, and felt too, powerless to resist.

> The mass and majesty of this world, all
> That carries weight and always weighs the same
> Lay in the hands of others; they were small
> And could not hope for help and no help came:
> What their foes liked to do was done, their shame
> Was all the worst could wish; they lost their pride
> And died as men before their bodies died.*

* W. H. Auden, *The Shield of Achilles.*

What would a decent alternative look like? D. H. Lawrence once put it nobly in these words:

> Men are free when they are in a living homeland, not when they are straying and breaking away ... Men are free when they belong to a living, organic, believing community, active in fulfilling some unfulfilled, perhaps unrealized purpose.

Just as we conceive violence, however, as an extreme condition and not as a social system, we never see loss of freedom in familiar terms, but in those of extreme histories and other countries. Violence is guns in the street and smashed windows; loss of freedom is jail and brutal policemen. To talk these days in Britain of production line work on the shop floor or the national institution of poverty as acts of violence is to mystify or antagonize one's audience. Yet so much of what we take for granted in our social experience should be intolerable to a free man. All that is intolerable is securely part of a totality of human relationships, and changing the intolerable means changing them. Advertising, like anything else, is part of those relationships. Inasmuch as it is clearly a commercial activity, it follows further that it is the product of those relationships which control and express our economics. As I have said, advertising is locked firmly into a total structure of communication systems. It follows again that it cannot be considered apart from all the ways in which men speak to men in our society. Since mass communications are themselves deeply influenced and often divided by commercial forces, we cannot logically consider them apart from the economic system which mobilizes them. Our final formulation in the syllogism is consequently a platitude: advertising is the offspring of capitalism. The study of advertising is therefore the study of an economic system in its symbolic forms.

That may be said impartially. Indeed the intention of this study is to provide procedures for the critical analysis of mass persuasion, irrespective of the tendency of the chosen examples. One may study *Oxfam* posters alongside Building Society copy or pet-food commercials on TV without being so humourless as to damn them all for acquisitiveness. But the main point about the study of advertising as of any other form of mass communication is that the study should help enlarge that area where we call ourselves our own men. We are imprisoned when we fail to recognize constraints upon our imagination. To perceive the constraints is to move them. The calculations of advertising are submarine; to dredge them out is an act of liberation. But the effort must be systematic. A general scepticism may be taken for granted: nobody *trusts* the adman; nobody admits to believing this or that commercial. What is lacking is an understanding of how values and production systems are bonded together by advertising codes; we have learned to talk about the precise relations between production system and product, between human relations and distribution, between consumption and crying need. The lack of such learning and such talk measures a critical lack of freedom. As things now are, a main effort towards the making of a free man's education must be the effort to understand how the masters of mass communication set out to hire and control people's lives. We shall draw the line back from an individual situation (advertising) to the structure of actions which made it possible. Every commercial carries the codes of its origins: the genetics of advertising are transmitted from the parent.

Mass communications

We live through the mass media as the main innovation in the social experience of the past thirty years. In our slatternly way, we take for granted the acceleration in the spread of television and broadcasting, and in the accompanying rise in literacy. At a time when all the political and consequently technological changes tend to isolate and specialize human activity, mass communications provide in a quite unprecedented way for universal contact and the exchange of information and images. To think about this state of affairs requires us again and sharply to think about these politics and their technology. It is hardly sensible to talk, like some prophets of a new world have done, of 'a global village', simply because we may watch on TV what is happening that night in Washington and Saigon. The social texture of village life was much denser and more vivid in its responses than we are likely to feel about televised life. The important point about television, radio and newsprint is that they provide almost our only commonly shared experiences and body of information. Anybody, even the most assiduous, can only acquire a very sketchy sense of what is happening. The information and the cultural life offered by mass communications is, of course, drastically calculated and selective, but it is the source from which we find out about our lives today. The system is enormously extended, and its technology is becoming more developed and available day by day. We must acknowledge that the control of the system rests firmly in a very few pairs of hands.

Where formerly communication was either spoken or written in local communities, the flow of information was reciprocal. The rise of literacy and the expansion of newsprint during the nineteenth century took place in contexts which still provided for the more gradual development and interplay of ideas and gave rise to a variety of dialogues, from the diverse contents of the intellectual journals of Victorian London to the dozens of broadsheets and newspapers available on the streets and in the inns of every small town. No doubt these publications were also in the hands of the entrepreneurs, but they were very numerous. In the present century the whole tendency of the economic system has been to surge centripetally into giant monopolies. The ownership of the mass communication system has sharply restricted itself. This momentum has intensified in the last twenty years in Britain which have seen the closure of the *Empire News*, the *News Chronicle*, the *Daily Herald*, the *Sunday Citizen* and the *Daily Sketch*, and a continual crisis at the presses of the *Guardian* and *The Times*. Seven out of eight national papers are now controlled by three publishing companies, and all of them derive the major part of their revenue from advertising. Along with mergers have gone similar concentrations in the local presses and in magazine ownership. In this situation it has seemed natural that when new television companies begin, their putative profits shall be auctioned behind locked doors and the decision as to who shall administer a local monopoly (Harlech, Tyne-Tees, Yorkshire, Thames) of information shall be taken by listening to the bids. And if we study the names in question, we shall see how securely the press, the entertainment and the commercial world interlock, and how comparatively few are the names which recur. The great American sociologist C. Wright Mills has made the necessary points about the U.S.A. and his description is largely transferable.

The pursuit of the moneyed life is the commanding value, in relation to which the influence of other values has declined, so men easily become morally ruthless in the pursuit of easy money and fast estate-building.

A great deal of American corruption—although not all of it—is simply a part of the old effort to get rich and then to become richer. But today the context in which the old drive must operate has changed. When both economic and political institutions were small and scattered ... no man had it in his power to bestow or to receive great favours. But when political institutions and economic opportunities are at once concentrated and linked, then public office can be used for private gain.

The men of the higher circles are not representative men; their high position is not the result of moral virtue; their fabulous success is not firmly connected with meritorious ability. Those who sit in the seats of the high and mighty are selected and formed by the means of power, the sources of wealth, the mechanics of celebrity, which prevail in their society. They are not men shaped by nationally responsible parties that debate openly and clearly the issues this nation now so unintelligently confronts. They are not men held in responsible check by a plurality of voluntary associations which connect debating publics with the pinnacles of decision. Commanders of power unequalled in human history, they have succeeded within the American system of organized irresponsibility.*

What we have then is a situation, which we take for granted, in which the control of an extremely expensive system is in the hands of those who most demand it. The commercial interests as a matter of survival must be in constant touch with a mass audience, and must constantly seek to manipulate that audience. Control of the communication system permits this. We then see the necessary means of universal communication adjusted in many unnoticed ways to the world-picture of the few controllers. They select the information which flows down the multiplicity of new channels, and consequently their commercial preoccupations mingle with, divert, alter, block and release all that flows with them.

Inasmuch as Western industry has driven the economic dynamism of the world for the past century, let us see how this inevitable cluster of interests has gathered. I have said that once upon a time social groups were tightly and locally based and more or less self-subsistent. The independent communities only linked loosely with others. The steady movement of people into towns, and the transformation of towns into centres of industrial production, accelerated one upon the other like gear wheels, and the development of mass communications helped to create a machine whose parts were specialized in the interests of production-line technology and in which no group was self-sufficient any longer. Mass communications are uniquely powerful in that no area of the society they serve can look after itself: each area

* *The Power Elite*, Oxford and New York, 1956, pp. 346, 361.

needs this form of contact. They derive yet more power from the changes within the dominant economics.

Since about 1918 the countries of Western Europe have been technically capable of eliminating poverty: that is to say, they are capable of producing the necessities of life in relative abundance for everybody. But the institutions of those societies depend on the continued existence of a poor (with their 'minimum wage') as the base against which the crucial conceptions of success, possession, promotion, and opportunity can be measured. This being so, the rich countries of the West have had to organize the distribution of abundance in such a way as to sustain their competitive inequalities. Since they are technically able to produce more or less what they like and since, further, their institutions forbid their members to produce enough of everything for everybody, they need to keep their production at the highest rates without reducing prices or consumption. With the constant injection of new investment from earlier surpluses (uninvested capital merely depreciates: the mattress stuffed with pound notes is eventually worthless) production is regularly increasing. The contradiction is then that to stay as rich you must produce more. And this compounds itself. But this process of increasing 'growth' (which we have all learned to desire) is itself deceptive. For the system cannot afford to glut itself on a given range of products: saturation must mean that the plant cannot run full out. It therefore follows that not only must production be kept at its highest, but that the *pattern* of products must constantly change. High production necessarily requires a high rate of consumption and this in turn requires a high rate of expendability and a rapid rate of change. The production must control and innovate what is consumed and in what quantities, and the quality and speeds of innovation vary the quality and speed of many important areas of people's lives. The apparent and bewildering choices facing a shopper today relate directly to critical changes in the rhythms of his life. What we need to ask—what is talked out elsewhere in this book—is what this abundance is worth in human terms, and what real scarcity is ignored by the mass consumer market. But the insistent choice of 'consumer' goods—i.e. in what we use, eat or wear out—is not only a necessary sequence in the production process, it has become deeply a part of our cultural habits. Changing habits of consumption have become dynamic in the lives of many people. Their habits and their expectations fluctuate inversely with the rhythms of the market. It is now a matter of moral need that there is a constantly rising standard of living; people need to spend and do not wish to save. The parameters of economic action not surprisingly define the lines of individual desire.

Obviously this description of human behaviour leaves out great tracts of complex wishes and intentions which have nothing to do with shopping. But even without any narrow and reductive view of how people behave we must understand that we learn our motives from our culture, and that much of what we casually think of as 'human nature' or 'instinct' is quite specific to a given social situation and is not all invariable. We *learn* prodigality or we learn thrift, and neither quality is innate. The genetics of an economic system are more powerful coders of how we behave than our biochemical inheritance. The system has taught us to spend, and to spend in certain ways. Of course there are pulls in contradictory directions, and (as we shall see) the effects of advertising are never simple even where they can be determined at all. There is no one-to-one model: 'we act this way *because of* this advertisement'. But the critical need for the expansion of plant and investment of capital in order to keep a particular system going has without any doubt created a form of behaviour which will maintain the system. No doubt human beings have always been liable to avarice, gluttony, rapaciousness and snobbery. But these drives have taken specific form beneath the pressure of advanced industrial capitalism and any judgements about wrong and right must take proper historical account of this fact. For that giant upheaval which we recognize as industrialism has destroyed the old and thick-textured local communities, and created a society whose relationships are much more loose-knit and transitory than ever before. Industrialism further created a system by which the human need to remain in communication with one's fellows could be satisfied in this unprecedented urban experience. Then the special nature of this industrialism required that it penetrate and organize the lines of communication to its own ends. We therefore find a people whose relative isolation and absence of lasting relationships make them urgently require human contact, unusually vulnerable to a system which, while it appears to provide a neutral means of contact, actually plans and shapes the kinds of contact possible. Industrialism, for survival on its own terms, had to make a dependent institution which would ensure an obedient consumer society. This institution is the advertising industry. It was the offspring of a productive machinery which had to transform areas of social living and social values without altering the distribution of wealth, power and prestige—indeed while consolidating them. The difficulty faced by this novel institution was to dispose of the rising income newly available after people had bought enough fuel, food and clothes. Attractively enough for advertisers and producers, the difficulty is self-perpetuating, for there are constantly rising levels of income within the dynamics of capital growth, and therefore a constant need to organize and appropriate the spare income. Advertising needs to direct this spare income towards given products and as more slack income becomes available, instantly to take this up tight by defining the acquired luxuries as a new base of 'necessities' from which to move on to the next level of expectation which has been constructed for the consumers. I don't at all want to impugn the drudgery cancelled by the widespread use of washing machines, but where once such appliances were rare luxuries, they are rapidly becoming accepted as 'necessities', and the next stage of expectation ('desire-level' in the market research cant) is becoming the washing-up machine. We can observe the same process not only amongst different domestic machines, but often within certain types of machinery. The most obvious example is the motor car, now almost universally defined as a social necessity. The producers' intention here must be to raise expectations about performance and finish so that the consumer will in the same way as before be encouraged to change vehicles in an insatiable search (he cannot, by definition, be satisfied) for a better car. The spiral growth and change is infinite: it projects into an infinite future invented for cash returns by the masters of production.

Of course the future must be predictable and it is the business of the advertising institution to make it predictable. The important point to grasp here is that predictability is not a short-lived matter of accurate market research with the prospects for a single product. We shall study this technique in Chapter Four. The institution must also generate a moral as well as an economic climate which controls attitudes towards consumption, modes of perception, linguistic conventions and changes. To sustain real inquiry into this process we must also notice how powerfully the ethics of advertising suffuse the whole system of communication. We must study not only the individual documents circulated by the producers but also how their information filters through our society, how the producers' ethics are refracted through quite other forms of behaviour. It would be an interesting exercise to study the astonishing success of the TV serial *The Forsyte Saga* and to note how completely the programme's moral atmosphere exhaled these ethics: an aspiration at once wistful and familiar towards the life style of the very rich; the ostentatious display of wealth and worldly success; the acquisition of objects (including beautiful women) in order to secure one's social identity. Such analysis is an essential part of understanding how mass communications mediate and enforce a certain structure of values, and these values derive from the needs of the economy. The analysis might go on to scrutinize the sort of information allowed to flow through the news channels, both in print and broadcasts. A useful example here is the treatment of the Vietnamese war about which the news media have simply excised a great deal of information on civilian deaths, poison bombing and the conditions of refugee camps, because these would call into question the bases of so much overseas investment by the big leviathan corporations. To propose such inquiry is not a matter of striking a simple revolutionary's posture. It is an invitation to *look and see*. How do mass communications group and interweave a national structure of values and attitudes? To answer that question requires the dissenter to open doors into many rooms: literary criticism, social psychology, sociology, politics, and to see how often these cross over their perspectives on the ground below. But the dissenter's inquiry cannot lose hold upon its middle, which is the human question, what do we know about ourselves? What means are there for finding it? What are we *allowed* to know? If we do not, with the specialist tools to hand, face those sharp questions, and reply to them in a human voice, there is no tolerable freedom, and no place to call our own. In a grim phrase, society has then become an adjunct of the economy.

Only our reason, strenuously exercised, can point how far along this road we have travelled. The operations of mass communication are not reasonable. They may be contradictory. Obviously there are men working the system who at times resist it, and criticize it audibly, either on a particular issue or in a more general way. By and large, however, the organism ramifies and extends itself by such devices as perpetuate its power. It creates men who will make it work, and it creates an ideology, as I consider in Chapter Three, to justify the men and that work. But the whole busy life of the organism is deeply irrational, as it has to be if it is to push consumption far beyond the limits of nausea, and its discourse is covert, its intentions hidden, and the whole management of its knowledge submarine and unconscious probably even to itself. For the conscience of the rich West is still not so enfeebled that it could not be appalled at its own inhumanity if it were made explicit. But the reasonable grounds for such self-knowledge are suppressed. If we believe in the need for truth about ourselves, it is our human duty to exhume these grounds and to meet the vast institutions of our society upon them.

Any society constructs new institutions to register and accommodate its changes. In one dimension, Western intellectual society invented the novel in which to take imaginative stock of its history in the nineteenth century; in another, a sector of the society constructed Trades Unions in response to the cruel demands made upon one social group by another. The most powerful and universal institution of this century is the mass communications system. In the past thirty years it has become the major innovation. It will not do to say that, for example, nuclear fission is a greater force, because the ends to which nuclear fission will be party depend overwhelmingly upon the identity of the controllers of the communications channels, and the information which they decide to release down them. Again, as witness the Vietnamese war, our response to mass destruction depends utterly on the language and information we possess with which to understand that destruction. Understanding mass communications is essential to the understanding of freedom and justice and equality, indeed to understanding any of the noble ideals for which men will strive. This system lies presently in a very limited number of hands and access to it is restricted in terms of the wealth and power which a man may possess. The system's influence is such that it is likely to dictate the movement of history in the foreseeable future. There seems no alternative institution which shows signs of counterposing a sufficient weight. Thus we have the likelihood that the drift of society will be recorded in the rhythms of economic expansion, consumption, reinvestment and expansion again, and that the moral life will discover itself in successive arrival at stages of relative consumer success and deprivation. The major institutions of Western society are capital, production, and communications. These three interlock at many levels. They work to maintain a consistent equipoise, and because the preferred expectations are, for all but the necessary poor, bewitching and sufficiently well upholstered, not many people are prepared to consider the alternative actions for which they perceive neither language nor opportunities. We have learned to accept responses as normal which if they were seen alertly we could only judge to be gross and distorted. We do not envisage another possibility.

In a just society, therefore, there would be some inequalities of status just as there would be some inequalities of class. But these would all be inequalities of status in the sense that Picasso has higher status as a painter than does an ungifted amateur, not the sense in which a duke has higher status than a labourer. Many people would look down on others; but this would be in the way that people are looked down on for being unmusical or clumsy or bad at football or even morally wicked, not the way in which they are looked down on for having black skins, or poor parents, or working-class accents. There would be many status-groups in the sense of people sharing a common style of life and perhaps common criteria of praise over wide areas of human activity. But there would not be status-strata, or castes, whose members could point to some socially institutionalized criterion for disrespecting, or being disrespected by, other people not sharing a common characteristic. Deference would be expressed by some people towards others; but this would be in the sense in which people defer to the opinions of those whom they believe to be wiser than themselves—the sense, in other words, which is synonymous with admiration. It would not be the sense in which labourer defers to the duke.

In the same way, there would be some educational inequalities in a just society. But no higher status would attach to any one branch of education except to the extent that those qualifying for it were all considered more deserving of praise. It might be that children receiving a longer or more specialized education than others would all share certain social characteristics; but these would be coincidental—they would not be the reasons for which an unequal education was being given to them. It is even possible that those receiving the most education would go into the better-rewarded occupations (assuming that these differentials were not overriden by claims of need); but those in the less well-paid jobs for which less education was necessary would have had an equal opportunity to choose this education, and would be less well rewarded only if their work was agreed to be less arduous, or to make less contribution towards the common welfare.*

The lack of such justice expresses itself in accents either frenzied and obscene, or stolid and suspicious; it is also tied in ways which the available information makes it very difficult to connect, with the much more visible and bloody restrictions on freedom in less physically comfortable parts of the world. The peasant families of Asia and Latin America, and these men and women in Gloucestershire link up:

* W. G. Runciman, *Relative Deprivation and Social Justice*, Routledge 1966, pp. 282–3.

The average forester of over twenty-five expects, when healthy, little of life . . . He expects to maintain what he has—job, family, home. He expects to continue to enjoy his pleasures—a cup of tea in bed, Sunday newspapers, the pub at weekends, an occasional trip to the nearest city or to London, some form of game, his jokes. His wife has her equivalent pleasures. Both of them have fantasies which are infinitely more resourceful and rich—perhaps particularly the wife, who ages far faster. They also have their opinions and their stories to tell, and these may cover much wider ground. But what they expect in their own situation in any foreseeable future is very little: they may want more, they may believe they have a right to more, but they have learned and they have been brought up to settle for a minimum. Life is like that they say.

Their foreseen minimum is not purely economic: it is not even principally economic: today the minimum might include a car. It is above all an intellectual, emotional and spiritual minimum . . . it substitutes the notion of endurance for that of experience, of relief for that of benefit.*

Here's confirmation of this diagnosis from a Mexican voice:

At one time I believed in a lot of things . . . now I believe in nothing. I wanted to see my village improve but with the passage of time I am convinced that it can't be done and no matter how saintly a public official may be when he takes office, he will accomplish nothing. Now I realize that in my village no one understands. We are blindfolded! All of us! Partly because of lack of culture, partly because of lack of unity and partly because of poverty . . . What is the good of my having ideas if I am a poor man? I cannot do a thing! . . . The new generation in my village has opened its eyes to other things but not to politics. When one talks about what is good for the *municipio* or for them, the young people don't come around to listen . . .

The peasants are ignorant and more than a little stupid.†

Any adequate theory of mass communications and the nature of advertising must build up from a sense of the interrelations between the converging histories of nations and their likely futures. There is nothing fatalist about these. There can be no religious belief either in apocalypse or in utopia; we can on the other hand only admit certain possibilities. Peasant and labourer are alike in that their situation is dictated by the need for an international system of vast monopolies to maintain capital investment, expansion and consumption. Such dictation is seen more visibly as violence when it is enforced by bullets, but it can work in subtler and doubtless more acceptable ways. To study these ways is to make a small effort for human freedom, but the

* John Berger, *A Fortunate Man*, Allen Lane, The Penguin Press, 1967, pp. 132–3.
† Oscar Lewis, *Pedro Martinez: A Mexican Peasant and His Family*, Random House Inc., 1964, pp. 454–5.

effort will only have meaning insofar as it is seen as part of a sporadic but world-wide attempt on the part of free men to take over the systems of production which hire out their lives. That is surely the great historical conflict which historians of the future—if there are any—will see to have been going on in these uneasy decades: the conflict between ownership from elsewhere and a shared and equal ownership on and of the ground. There is no saying at this stage who will be victorious, but change can only come through existing or spontaneously created social institutions. It cannot, that is, take place without prior organization and without an institution to match the might of the opposition. For example, the main social experience for Britain of the past forty years was the war. Under the impulse of this drastic social event, society changed drastically. But this could only happen through the most powerful social institutions of the time—the Forces. Insofar as these had to dissolve their hitherto rigid caste system, English society received a powerful dose of egalitarianism which spread through many sectors. After the war all kinds of stabilizing and anaesthetic nostrums were applied and the groundswell of change died away. Society went on changing, but the source of energy returned to a few men. As things are, the main social institution with the specific gravity to balance against the power of mass communications over the social knowledge which is the essential energy of change is education. This is no simple equation. Education versus the media. The schools, universities and colleges are too intimately bonded with the communications structure for the resultant impulse of society to be discoverable by taking moments about the twin forces of education and the mass media. Their attitudes one to another are profoundly ambivalent and calculating. Yet there is no doubt that in this situation the teachers need an altogether more coherent and radical theory of mass communications and how they work than is generally available. The point of departure may well be advertising. There has been widespread and piecemeal criticism of advertising in education ever since F. R. Leavis's and Denys Thompson's school textbook *Culture and Environment* came out in the 1930s. As I have said, the criticism has lacked a coherent theory and justification beyond such reach-me-down bromides as 'we must teach them to think for themselves: there's plenty will take their money off them if we don't'. Nonetheless we must begin where we share something. I have tried in this chapter to offer a general theory of mass communications placed in the dominating context of their economic controls and intentions. Advertising, I have emphasized, is a function of mass communications. What is now in place is a general critique of advertising which will not only shape the subsequent chapters but also offer a miniature model of the communications system in an advanced technology. If people accept this model, they can perhaps project it into the far vaster social and political explanations from which it derives. That is to say I hope that this account of advertising will stand as an account of very much more; that it will illuminate whole other areas of our lives and of the economic processes which control and divide our worlds; most crucially, that it will establish the presence of connections between different kinds of work, in factories, in teaching, at home, which we have falsely learned to think of as separate. To think straight about advertising—which does not mean thinking in crude or satanic colours—might be to get straight about much of that language, morality and action of our lives which we choose from confectioneries arranged by others for their profit.

The social meanings of advertising

Social realities do not form themselves by natural laws. They are prepared and interpreted by people. At present a small and powerful minority completes almost all the preparation and interpretation which is commonly shared. The definition of the *word* requires that the mass media mediate social realities: they continuously describe society and of necessity the description is selective and shaped. We do not have to believe in any conspiracies to see how crucial it is to hopes of a common and equal culture that there be commonly reliable descriptions of social reality, since so much of life must now for all of us be a matter of reports from other places.

Control of mass communication means control of what people know, and the forms in which they know it. Insofar as the media are controlled by commercial interests, then the management and presentation of knowledge will inevitably be loaded with various implications. Nor can we have much doubt that the first intention of a newspaper or of commercial television is to gain advertising revenue. Nicholas

Kaldor's classic study* made the proportion of revenue derived from advertising public over twenty years ago, and the regular crisis of the papers with circulations below one million is permanent evidence of their chronic ailment. (Not that the condition is inevitable, as the stringently independent and fourpenny *Le Monde* shows.) The profit-making intentions of the independent television companies were never in question: the lobby was formed to that end, and bid accordingly. Mass communications judge themselves by the cost-effective criteria: profitability, capital-intensive plant, productivity, and the imminence of local commercial radio and the introduction of management consultancy at the BBC make it clear how unremitting the pressures of these criteria are. In this way advertising revenue comes to be the indispensable source of capital to the system, and the terms of politics and culture and those of the plain blunt man's market-place economics are forever interwined and sophisticated. A newspaper's relation to its advertising backers therefore varies according to its circulation and its readers' social habits. But all newspapers, like ITV and magazines, sustain their readership in the terms which their main commercial sponsors can accept. This is not likely to mean that a particular organization will try to dictate editorial policy on some line or other, but rather the much more elusive result that the topic and tone of a publication will be deeply coloured by its place within the commercial structure. The loss of this or that advertising client is no doubt important to a TV network or newspaper, but must happen sometimes in the normal competitive run of things. What, for the sake of its survival, cannot happen is a wholesale movement away of a kind caused by a disconcerting change in editorial style. But then this is very improbable. What we find instead is the harmonious interaction of advertising and editorial styles, styles which consistently reproduce and endorse the consumers' way of life. It is the easy presumption of this style which is so telling, for the manner never really admits of contraversion, as the analysis in Chapter Four suggests. For the style is also a code of manners and, it follows, a structure of values. The values transpire in the objects named and illustrated, and in which they are possessed. Simply put, the central values are extreme wealth, sexual attractiveness and rapacity, and competitive success. Attainment of the values is signalled by acquiring the appropriate objects, using them,

* N. Kaldor and R. Silverman, *Advertising Expenditure and Revenue of the Press*, Cambridge, 1948.

throwing them away and acquiring replacements. Continuous and conspicuous consumption is the driving energy of this fiction. The point is not that there is no need to aspire to the possession of objects: it would be an open insult to many women to claim that electric irons or automatic washing machines had not liberated them for more enjoyment and left them with more energy. The emphasis of advertising is not laid on such obvious human relief; rather, the objects advertised are drenched in a certain light and smell. They give off the powerful fragrance of the very rich and instead of leaving the object in an intelligible domestic world, remove it to a fantastic one. Not that it is only commodities which are advertised. The advertisements studied in Chapter Four put out by big corporations in the cultivation of an 'image' fit snugly into the atmosphere. The word 'image' which means both an insubstantial picture thrown forward from a projector and a magical vision of a supernatural power is a word with an ironic cutting edge.

What the styles of advertising do is tie the human behaviour which subtends the economic system to the human needs we all feel. Extravagance, greed, careless waste, prodigal consumption, needless change, become both the means to and the experience of imperious human wants: to love and be loved, to be safe, to be at home, to have friends, to be wise, to command one's life. At the same time the circle of advertising information is tightly closed to the intervention of such questions as 'Who goes short while you produce more?' 'Do we need what you produce?' 'Who pays for you anyway?' Such questions cannot of course be asked, because it is the nature of total systems that they close the circle against alternatives. This is what totalitarianism means. For

the whole concept of democracy is bound up with this concept of rational argument, and the democratic concept of equality is partly to be elucidated with reference to the fact that rational argument appeals to criteria which entail a verdict that is irrespective of persons. If, however, I change your views by giving you injections, or by causal manipulation of any other kind, then I destroy this equality, for I see you as manipulated, myself as manipulator.*

What advertising must therefore do to close the circle against reason (which is impossible) is to embody in as anodyne, non-rational a way as it can the structure of values by which the parent society lives. Then

* A. C. MacIntyre, 'A Mistake about Causality in Social Science', in P. Laslett and W. G. Runciman, eds., *Politics, Philosophy and Society*, 2nd series, Blackwell, 1962, p. 68.

if challenged by reason it can point to the way in which it encourages that structure to thrive. Thus, it offers itself as satisfying our primary wants but further as satisfying them in approved ways. That is, the implicit moral language of advertising sanctions individual freedom, defined as the unimpeded exercise of a competitive initiative and free choice. But these virtues are revalued. 'Initiative' and 'free choice' genuinely exercised would profoundly subvert the smooth running of oligopolies. Instead these primary virtues are offered as fulfilling themselves by mass purchase and mass consumption. Choice and initiative are so demoralized (it is the right word) that they retain no human energy. Initiative in this context has no moral motive: it is revised as acquisitiveness. Choice is not the action of an alert and free sensibility so much as the trained reflex of an organism instructed to react to the provided alternatives, but never to dispute their nature nor to argue for better provisions. We talk about freedom of choice without perceiving what alternatives remain neglected or suppressed and without naming actual suffering and scarcity. There are critical freedoms which simply do not exist, and the choices we can make are limited in number and largely empty of social significance.

The function of advertising was first to organize and control people's behaviour in the interests of predictable capital growth, surplus and reinvestment. It has now become the dynamic of a communications system articulated about this common centre, gradually excluding the contrary flows of energy which a wider rationality releases. In turn, advertising derives its own energy from the economic system. It is now necessary to look closer at the economics of advertising—not, that is, the economic system which contains advertising, which is described in this first chapter, but the economic behaviour of advertising itself.

TWO

The Economics of Advertising

PART I

In the arguments about advertising a main plank in the opposition case has been that expenditure on advertising represents a shocking waste, and the traditional rejoinder has been that the expenditure is necessary for the controlled, stable expansion of productivity and technical progress. Chapter Three documents in detail the ideology of the advertising industry, but it is first necessary to look at the economic grounds for the folklore of both critics and defenders of the system, though it is always necessary to remember that in a general analysis advertising is a symptom of a damnable social failure: a failure to construct a communications system in public hands and without constraints. It will be to the point to assemble here a selection of significant details from the brute statistics which are randomly available in the press and trade journals.

TABLE I   NATIONAL EXPENDITURE ON DIRECT OR 'RAW' ADVERTISING

U.S.A. annual expenditure on direct advertising 1970	\$20,000 million
(i.e. \$89·56 per head of total population)	
U.K. annual expenditure on direct advertising 1970	\$1,250 million or £520 million
(i.e. \$21·31 or £8.18.0 per head of total population)	

N.B. These totals do not take into account the costs of packaging, which, in a very crude sum, are estimated at about another \$25,000 million in the U.S.A. and about £670 million in the United Kingdom nor do they take into account the costs of market research, which are incalculable.

SOURCE: *Marketing/Communications (U.S.A.) Projections*, March 1970.

TABLE 2

The following organizations spend these sums on TV and press advertising for their clients in this country:

	1968	1969	% change
J. Walter Thompson (subsidiary of U.S. firm with billings $740m in 1969) Customers in 1970 Guinness, Brooke Bond, Oxo	£19·8m	£22·3m	+13
Masius Wynne-Williams (largest British-owned firm, with 13 subsidiaries outside U.K.; group billings in 1969, £47m). Customers Wills, Mars Petfood, Wilkinsons	£17·9m	£18·5m	+6
Ogilvy and Mather (subsidiary of Ogilvy, Benson & Mather, New York; group billing in 1969, $230m). Customers include Gillette, Shell, Egg Marketing	£12·8m	£12·8m	—
Young and Rubicam (subsidiary of U.S. firm with group billings in 1969, $523m). Customers include Daz, Heinz	£10·1m	£11·6m	+15
Hobson Bates (merged with U.S. firm in 1959; group billings in 1969, $375m). Customers include Procea and Max Factor	£10·8m	£10·7m	−2
Lintas (formerly owned by Unilever; now 49% of shares held in U.S. agency S.S.C. and B. billing $300m)	£9·0m	£10·5m	+16
Leo Burnett—LPE (part U.S. owned, part London Press Exchange). Customers include Cadbury, Giro, Alka-Seltzer	£10·0m	£10·6m	+6
Wasey Pritchard Wood and Quadrant (formed in 1969; U.S. owned (American Interpublic))		£9·5m	—
S. H. Benson (British owned, in trading partnership with U.S. firm Needham, Harper Steers). Customers include Rowntrees, Johnny Walker	£9·0m	£9·5m	+5
Collett, Dickenson, Pearce & Partners (British owned; no U.S. trading partnership). Customers include Aer Lingus, Whitbread	£5·9m	£7·7m	+30
McCann-Erikson (subsidiary of U.S. firm, American Interpublic; billing $511m in 1969; A.I. also own Wasey Pritchard Wood and Quadrant)	£5·5m	£6·5m	+18

TABLE 2 *continued*

	1968	1969	% change
Dorland (U.S. trading partnership; British owned). Customers include Heinz, Bass, Pirelli	£7·5m	£7·6m	+1
Foote Cone & Belding (subsidiary of U.S. firm with total billing of $253m). Customers include Rootes, I.C.I. Paints	£5·5m	£4·9m	−11
Garland–Compton (British owned). Customers include Rowntrees Fruit Gums and Pastilles, Fairy Snow	£4·0m	£4·8m	+20
Benson and Bowles (subsidiary of U.S. firm Lambe & Robinson; billing $225m in 1969)	£3·5m	£4·4m	+26

SOURCE: *Times Business News* and *Advertising Supplement*, 14 May 1970.

TABLE 3   ADVERTISEMENT REVENUE—1968 TO (JAN–MARCH) 1970

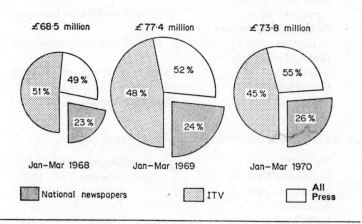

The Times, 14 May 1970.

TABLE 4

4A. The following products were launched or sustained by individual promotion campaigns costing these sums at various times during 1968–69–70.

Promotion (i.e. 'point of sale' and media advertising)
Campaigns

Evo-stik adhesive	£40,000	(*Times*, 29 October 1969)
Quosh orange drink	£200,000	(*Times*, 4 June 1969)
Kenwood Mini-mixer	£125,000	(*Times*, 4 June 1969)
Daily Mirror Magazine	£500,000	(*Times*, 4 June 1969)
Rootes *Avenger*	£400,000	(*Warwick University Ltd.,* Penguin 1970, p. 14)
Ford *Capri*	£270,000	(*Times*, 8 October 1969)
Godfrey Davis Rail Drive	£80,000	(*Times*, 8 October 1969)
I.C.I. 'Pathfinder' Series (Image-building)	£160,000	(*Times*, 14 January 1970)
Save & Prosper Unit Trust	£1,3000,000	(*Times*, 4 February 1970)
Bio-Strath Tonic	£80,000	(*Times*, 21 January 1970)
Lyons Tours Package Holidays	£250,000	(*Times*, 19 November 1970)
Libby McNeill & Libby 'Label Bonanza'	£150,000	(*Times*, 29 April 1970)
Post Office Corporation off-peak telephone calls	£150,000	(*Times*, 22 October 1969)
I.P.C. *Woman's Own*	£170,000	(*Times*, 22 October 1969)
Knorr Soups (booster programme)	£200,000	(*Campaign*, 26 June 1970)
Gibbs Signal Toothpaste (aimed at children)	£350,000	(*Campaign*, 26 June 1970)
Bristol-Myers 'Mum' deodorant	£200,000	(*Campaign*, 12 June 1970)
United Bakeries New Slimming Bread	£100,000	(*Campaign*, 15 May 1970)

4B. *Annual Accounts* (i.e. continuous support of existing products)

Vat 69 Whisky	£70,000	(*Campaign*, 3 July 1970)
Courtaulds 'Courtelle'	£150,000	(*Campaign*, 3 July 1970)
Hennessy Cognac	£100,000	(*Times*, 14 January 1970)
All alcoholic drinks	£27,000,000	(*Times*, 23 June 1969)
Lyons Maid Ice-Cream	£1,000,000	(*Campaign*, 26 June 1970)
Avis Rent-a-car	£300,000	(*Campaign*, 26 June 1970)

TABLE 4 *continued*

4b. *Annual Accounts—cont.*

Fray Bentos TV campaign in 1969 on individual profits	£300,000	(*Campaign*, 26 June 1970)
H.M. Government	£4,600,000	1 January–31 May 1970 (*Campaign*, 12 June 1970)
Rank Hovis McDougall Flour	£272,000	(*Campaign*, 5 June 1970)
B. Rail, S. Region	£150,000	(*Campaign* 5 June 1970)
All Unit Trusts in 1969	£3,280,000	(*Campaign*, 5 June 1970)
All Unit Trusts in 1970	£36,400	(*Campaign*, 5 June 1970)
Pyrex	£200,000	(*Campaign*, 22 May 1970)
Playtex swimwear	£1,000,000	(*Times*, 12 August 1970)
Shelter	£50,000	(*Campaign*, 12 June 1970)

SOURCES: *Times Business News* and *Campaign* (formerly World's Press News) weekly, Haymarket Press, 9 Harrow Road, W.2. See also *Market Research* (photostat), and *The Advertising Directory 1969*, 4 vols, photostat; confidential to subscriber: Vol. 1—*Products and Promotions* (an alphabetical list of 14,000 products, giving agency and estimates of press and TV expenditure in 1968; Vol. 2—*Agencies and Advertisers* (800 agencies, list of accounts, etc.); Vol. 3—*Manufacturers and Distributors*; Vol. 4—*Annual Statistical Review* (225 product *groups* (with details of products in each group) with manufacturer, agent, estimates of expenditure on TV and press advertising). See also *Marketing Forum*, Institute of Marketing, Richbell Place, London WC1.

TABLE 5   WHERE ADVERTISING MONEY IS SPENT

	1965	1966	1967	1968	1965	1966	1967	1968
		£m				Percentage of total		
Press								
Display	172	171	165	179	40	39	37	36
Classified	66	71	72	87	15	16	16	18
Financial	7	7	7	10	2	2	2	2
Trade and Technical Journals	39	41	41	44	9	9	9	9
Total press	284	290	285	320	66	66	64	65
Television	106	109	124	132	25	25	27	27
Other media	41	41	41	42	9	9	9	8
Total	431	440	450	494	100	100	100	100

TABLE 5   *continued*

	1965	1966	1967	1968	1965	1966	1967	1968
		£m				Percentage of total		
Which press media								
National news-								
papers	88	88	84	99	20	20	19	20
Regional news-								
papers	87	87	87	99	20	20	19	20
Magazines	48	50	46	50	12	12	10	10
Trade and								
technical	39	41	41	44	9	9	9	9
Other publications	4	5	7	8	1	1	2	2
Production costs	18	19	20	20	4	4	5	4
Total press	284	290	285	320	66	66	64	65

	1961	1962	1963	1964	1965	1966	1967	1968
Total advertising expenditure	340	349	370	414	431	440	450	494

	1961	1962	1963	1964	1965	1966	1967	1968
Total as a percentage of consumers' expenditure	1·9	1·8	1·8	1·9	1·9	1·8	1·8	1·8

	1961	1962	1963	1964	1965	1966	1967	1968
Total as a percentage of Gross National Product	1·4	1·4	1·4	1·4	1·4	1·3	1·3	1·4

SOURCE: *The Times*, 4 July 1969, quoting *Advertising Statistics Working Party Report*, 1969.

Of this expense, £234m went on branded consumer goods, and the rest was scattered amongst government, industrial, trade and technical, and classified advertising. It has already been pointed out that packaging far more than doubles this expenditure (see Table 1). The figure 1·4 per cent (or 3·3 per cent if we include packaging) of the Gross National Product is given some comparative scale by quoting the 4·9 per cent which was spent on the national health service in 1969, and the 0·39 per cent given in overseas aid. A reasonable guess might estimate market research at another 1·5 per cent of the Gross National Product.

TABLE 6A   NEWSPAPER ADVERTISING

Proportions of total revenue attributable to circulation and advertising*

Class of newspaper		1964 %	1967 %	1969 (estimated) %
Dailies:				
The Times The Guardian Telegraph	Circulation Advertising	24 75	29 70	27 72
Mirror Mail Sketch Express The Sun	Circulation Advertising	56 43	65 34	61 38
Sundays:				
Sunday Times Sunday Telegraph Observer	Circulation Advertising	20 79	23 76	23 76
Sunday Mirror People Sunday Express News of the World	Circulation Advertising	56 44	59 41	59 40

NOTE: One per cent of total revenue comes from other sources.
    * National Board for Prices and Incomes, Report No. 141: *Costs and Revenue of National Newspapers*, H.M.S.O., 1970, p. 3.

TABLE 6B   REVENUE OF NATIONAL NEWSPAPERS

Sales and advertising revenue 1964–69, £000's

Dailies:	The Times, Telegraph, Guardian			Mirror, Mail, Sketch, Express, Sun			ALL
	Sales	Advertising	Total*	Sales	Advertising	Total*	Total*
1964	5,387	16,848	22,431	37,696	28,773	67,149	89,580
1965	6,703	19,429	26,338	43,012	28,247	71,804	98,142
1966	6,948	18,803	25,978	44,708	24,906	70,236	96,214
1967	7,464	18,361	26,047	45,722	23,576	70,035	96,082
1968	9,068	22,750	32,046	52,949	27,365	80,974	113,020
1969 (est.)	9,232	24,581	34,149	52,905	32,882	86,226†	120,375

Sundays:	Sunday Times, Sunday Telegraph, Observer			Sunday Mirror, Sunday Express, News of the World, People			ALL
	Sales	Advertising	Total*	Sales	Advertising	Total*	Total*
1964	2,585	10,103	12,779	18,285	14,380	32,858	45,637
1965	2,857	11,748	14,731	17,611	13,489	31,290	46,021
1966	3,246	12,933	16,319	17,768	12,915	30,857	47,176
1967	3,990	13,522	17,692	18,727	12,949	31,883	49,575
1968	4,703	15,863	20,705	20,950	14,414	35,562	56,267
1969 (est.)	5,127	17,023	22,315	22,465	15,240	37,899	60,214

SOURCE: N.B.P.I. Report 141, loc.cit., p. 33.
* Total revenue includes other revenue.
† Including the *Sun* at its 1968 level of revenue.

TABLE 6C REVENUE AND COSTS OF NATIONAL NEWSPAPERS EXPRESSED
IN PENCE PER COPY SOLD (BEFORE DECIMALIZATION)

	Dailies		Sundays	
	Quality	Popular	Quality	Popular
Number of Newspapers	3	5	3	4
	d	d	d	d
Revenue and cost per copy				
Sales revenue	3·40	3·27	7·06	4·66
Advertising revenue	8·53	1·69	23·81	3·21
Other revenue	0·09	0·04	0·21	0·04
Total revenue	12·02	5·01	31·08	7·91
Newsprint and ink	3·54	1·51	7·82	2·35
Circulation and distribution	1·32	0·38	4·81	0·78
Total newsprint and distribution	4·86	1·89	12·63	3·13
Production costs	3·74	1·35	9·35	2·10
Editorial costs	1·98	0·77	4·26	0·89
Administrative costs	1·14	0·45	1·93	0·62
Other fixed costs	0·81	0·15	2·53	0·25
Total editorial and overheads	3·93	1·37	8·72	1·76
Total costs	12·53	4·61	30·70	6·99
Profit	−0·51	0·40	0·38	0·92
Size of paper	Pages	Pages	Pages	Pages
Advertising	11·4	4·3	28·5	10·1
Editorial	15·6	8·3	25·2	11·5
Total	27·0	12·6	53·7	21·6
Space devoted to advertising*	42%	34%	53%	46%

SOURCE: N.B.P.I. Report 141, p. 34.
* Cf. *Le Monde*, 16.6% display ad., 22% classified; *N.Y. Herald Tribune*, 15.4% display ad., 3% classified.

TABLE 7　NEWSPAPER ADVERTISING: A SELECTION OF THE RATES PAID
AUGUST (1970)

7A. *Daily Mirror**

Back page solus	$6\frac{3}{4}'' \times 3\frac{1}{16}''$	£730
$\frac{1}{4} \times 3$ columns centre spread	$3\frac{3}{8}'' \times 4\frac{5}{8}''$	£524
Solus page 2	$6\frac{3}{8}'' \times 4\frac{5}{8}''$	£1,000
Solus page 2	$10\frac{1}{8}'' \times 4\frac{5}{8}''$	£1,504
Solus page 3	$6\frac{3}{4}'' \times 4\frac{5}{8}''$	£1,000
$\frac{3}{4} \times 3$ centre spread	$10\frac{1}{8}'' \times 4\frac{5}{8}''$	£1,572
3 columns centre spread	$13\frac{1}{2}'' \times 4\frac{5}{8}''$	£2,096
Full page, right-hand	$13\frac{1}{2}'' \times 10\frac{15}{16}''$	£4,390

7B. *News of the World**

Full page	$22'' \times 9$ columns	£8,448
Budget page	$18'' \times 9$ columns, solus	£7,000
Budget page	$17'' \times 9$ columns	£6,600
Mini page	$13'' \times 7$ columns	£4,150
Half page	$11'' \times 9$ columns	£4,224
Half page	$11'' \times 9$ columns, r.h. page, main feature spread	£4,400
$5\frac{1}{2}'' \times 2$ columns, front page, semi solus		£750
$5\frac{1}{2}'' \times 2$ columns, back page, semi solus		£750

7C. *Guardian**

Standard rate per single column inch		£10
Whole page	$22\frac{1}{4}'' \times 15\frac{1}{4}''$	£1,780
$15'' \times 6$ columns	$15'' \times 11\frac{3}{8}''$	£900
$\frac{1}{2}$ page	$11\frac{1}{8}'' \times 15\frac{1}{4}'''$	£890
4 columns	$22\frac{1}{4}'' \times 7\frac{9}{16}'''$	£890
$13'' \times 5$ columns	$13'' \times 9\frac{1}{2}''$	£650
$11'' \times 4$ columns	$11'' \times 7\frac{9}{16}''$	£440
$11'' \times 3$ columns	$11'' \times 5\frac{5}{8}''$	£330
$8'' \times 2$ columns	$8'' \times 3\frac{3}{4}''$	£160
$6'' \times 2$ columns	$6'' \times 3\frac{3}{4}''$	£120

Special 10 per cent premium are payable for particular pages, e.g. front or
leader-facing pages.

---

* SOURCES: *Daily Mirror* Advertising Department, 33 Holborn, E.C.1. *News of the World*, Advertising Office, 30 Bouverie St E.C.4, *Guardian* Advertising Dept, 21 John St, W.C.1.

TABLE 8A ITV ADVERTISING RATES—THAMES TV† EFFECTIVE (OCTOBER 1970)

Basic Spot Advertising Rates

	7 secs £	15 secs £	30 secs £	45 secs £	60 secs £
Monday to Thursday					
Up to 4.00 p.m.	35	60	85	125	170
4.00–5.00	95	170	240	360	480
5.00–6.00	200	350	500	750	1,000
6.00–6.55	320	560	800	1,200	1.600
6.55–10.30	640	1,120	1,600	2,400	3,200
6.55–10.30*	600	1,050	1,500	2,250	3,000
Monday/Wednesday/Thursday					
10.30–11.25 p.m.	320	560	800	1,200	1,600
11.25–12.00	160	280	400	600	800
12.00–close	35	60	85	125	170
Tuesday					
10.30–10.50 p.m.	240	420	600	900	1,200
10.50–12.00	120	210	300	450	600
12.00–close	35	60	85	125	170
Friday					
Up to 4.00 p.m.	35	60	85	125	170
4.00–5.00	95	170	240	360	480
5.00–6.00	240	420	600	900	1,200
6.00–7.00	350	615	880	1,320	1,760

Thames TV special rates for 'Winter Holiday Time' ads by travel agencies ('53,620 brochures requested last year').

Package 1: basic length 30 seconds.

A complete theme sequence lasting up to 3½ minutes. The commercials appear after a mood-setting opening scene, and are followed by a short closing announcement telling viewers how to obtain their brochures.

30 seconds	Each
One spot in any one week	£1,200
Two or more spots in any one week	£1,130
45 seconds	Each
One spot in any one week	£1,800
Two or more spots in any one week	£1,695

SOURCE: Thames Television Ltd, Kingsway, W.C.2.

* Special rate for early bookings. This lower rate will apply to all bookings made at least eight weeks before transmission.

† Times as cited by the companies in Tables 8A–C.

TABLE 8B   ITV ADVERTISING RATES—TYNE-TEES TV (COMBINED NOVEMBER 1971
WITH YORKSHIRE TV AS TRIDENT)

Basic Spot Advertising Rates—Effective from 5 October 1970

	7 secs £	15 secs £	30 secs £	45 secs £	60 secs £
Weekdays					
Up to 5.00 p.m.	Off-peak G.H.I.'s at 30p per thousand				
5.00–5.45	35	55	75	115	150
5.45–6.25	55	85	120	180	240
6.25–7.00	85	135	190	285	380
7.00–10.25 (peak time)	120	185	265	400	530
10.25–10.40	95	145	210	315	420
10.40–11.30	60	90	130	195	260
11.30–close (exc. Fridays)	20	30	40	60	80
11.30–close (Fridays only)	35	55	80	120	160
Saturday					
Up to 3.00 p.m.	10	15	20	30	40
3.00–4.00	25	40	60	90	120
4.00–5.40	50	80	115	175	230
5.40–6.50	70	110	155	235	310
6.50–10.00 (peak time)	90	140	200	300	400
10.00–11.30	75	120	170	255	340
11.30–close	50	75	110	165	220

SOURCE: Tyne-Tees Television Ltd, TV Centre, City Road, Newcastle, NE1 2AL.
N.B. In the year ending April 1969 the Tyne-Tees income from advertisements totalled
£4,560,095. From this, £756,179 was paid in television advertising levy. The Chancellor
cut back the levy sharply in 1971.

TABLE 8C   ITV ADVERTISING RATES—LONDON WEEKEND TV

London Weekend Television: Autumn Rate Card 1970— Effective 2 October 1970

	7 secs £	15 secs £	30 secs £	45 secs £	60 secs £
Friday					
19.00–23.00	620	1,120	1,600	2.400	3,200
19.00–23.00†	580	1,050	1,500	2,250	3,000
23.00–23.55	310	560	800	1,200	1,600
23.55–close	120	210	300	450	600

* Guaranteed Home Impacts.   † See over.

EARNS $25,000 A YEAR...

...but he's heading for *failure*

YOU'D SAY that Mr. A has *everything*. Two big cars. A fine home. A lovely wife. Happy children with their rosy futures seemingly certain. Yet . . . the picture could change *overnight*. His family's security could be *swept away* . . . because he has not planned properly for tomorrow.

RNS $100 A WEEK...

...and he's heading for *success*

R. B, at $100 a week, is already car-rked for success. For he knows where stands today . . . what's more, he knows ere he is going tomorrow. With an » to the future he has drawn his own *alagraph* plan . . . a plan that provides ply for his family's tomorrow . . . yet mits comfortable living today.

Don't guess about your future... *Analagraph it!*

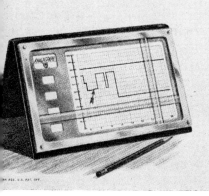

■ Why leave *your* family's future to chance? With the *Analagraph* . . . created by The Mutual Benefit . . . you can *see* what's ahead. And it takes only 30 minutes to chart a plan that lets *you* enjoy good living today . . . and spells security for your loved ones' tomorrows.

■ You chart your own goals . . . protection for your family . . . education for your children . . . a debt-free home . . . funds for retirement.

■ The *Analagraph* is exclusive with The Mutual Benefit. It is offered as part of our service without cost or obligation. Write today for the interest-ing new booklet, "The Analagraph—What It Can Do For You".

P.S. *Where estate problems are complex, your Mutual Benefit representative will cooperate with your legal adviser and the trust officer of your bank to assure maximum security for you and your family.*

THE MUTUAL BENEFIT
LIFE INSURANCE COMPANY

ORGANIZED IN 1845 NEWARK, NEW JERSEY

Plate 2. Advertisement reproduced in Marshall
McLuhan, *The Mechanical Bride*

Plate 3. Postcard Pop Art Dress

TABLE 8C *continued*

	7 secs £	15 secs £	30 secs £	45 secs £	60 secs £
Saturday					
Up to 16.00*	—	175	250	375	500
16.00–18.00	270	490	700	1,050	1,400
18.00–18.45	350	630	900	1,350	1,800
18.45–22.25	620	1,120	1,600	2,400	3,200
18.45–22.25†	540	980	1,400	2,100	2,800
23.20–close	135	245	350	525	700
Sunday					
Up to 19.20	—	265	375	565	750
19.20–19.35	310	560	800	1,200	1,600
19.35–23.00	620	1,120	1,600	24,00	3,200
19.35–23.00†	580	1,050	1,500	2,250	3,000
23.00–close	310	560	800	1,200	1,600

SOURCE: London Weekend Television, 25–28 Old Burlington St, W.1.

* Time up to 16.00 on Saturday afternoon will be sold by means of a Guaranteed Audience Scheme. Guaranteed Home Impacts only will be sold and the rates per half million are as shown above. Children's products will, when possible, be slotted near children's programmes.

The rate is guaranteed at a maximum cost per thousand home impacts per 30 seconds of 50 p.

† Special rate for early bookings.

TABLE 9A   THE MASS MARKET

Network Top Twenty   *Week ended 14 September 1969*

Programme	Originator	Homes viewing
Who-Dun-It	ATV	7·35 millions
The Best Things in Life	ATV	6·95 millions
Public Eye	Thames	6·65 millions
News at Ten (Wednesday)	ITN	6·65 millions
News at Ten (Tuesday)	ITN	6·30 millions
Coronation Street (Monday)	Granada	6·25 millions
Coronation Street (Wednesday)	Granada	5·90 millions
Never Mind the Quality, Feel the Width	Thames	5·90 millions
You've made your Bed, Now Lie In It	Anglia	5·70 millions
News at Ten (Thursday)	ITN	5·65 millions
World in Action	Granada	5·60 millions
Doctor in the House	London Weekend	5·60 millions
News at Ten (Monday)	ITN	5·50 millions
Softly, Softly	BBC	5·50 millions
Not in Front of the Children	BBC	5·35 millions
The Jimmy Tarbuck Show	ATV	5·30 millions
Opportunity Knocks!	Thames	5·25 millions
This Week	Thames	5·20 millions
Dick Van Dyke	BBC	5·20 millions
Dad's Army	BBC	5·15 millions
Wojeck	BBC	5·15 millions
The Frankie Howerd Show	ATV	5·15 millions

* SOURCE: Produced for Joint Industry Committee for Television Advertising Research (JICTAR) by Audits of Great Britain Ltd (AGB) in *ITV* 1970.

TABLE 9B NATIONAL DAILY NEWSPAPERS—AVERAGE DAILY CIRCULATION (000's)

Newspaper	1958	1959	1960	1961	1962	1963	1964	1965	1966	1967	1968	1969
Daily Telegraph	1,117*	1,155*	1,191*	1,250*	1,261*	1,305†	1,319	1,344	1,353	1,392	1,393	1,380
Guardian	178	186	206	240	263	264	275	273	281	285	275	291
The Times	248	254	262	257	254	254	256	256	282	349	408	432
Daily Mirror	4,527	4,521	4,607	4,578	4,610	4,737	5,018	4,988	5,132	5,252	4,992	4,964
Daily Mail	2,105	2,078	2,445	2,649	2,548	2,476	2,412	2,444	2,318	2,168	2,067	1,976
News Chronicle	1,255*	1,207*	1,162*	—	—	—	—	—	—	—	—	—
Daily Herald/The Sun	1,513	1,466	1,412	1,407	1,348	1,311	1,265	1,317	1,238	1,146	1,038	951‡
Daily Sketch	1,213	1,154	1,096	991	954	928	855	835	857	879	900	871
Daily Express	4,063	4,091	4,206	4,321	4,288	4,271	4,233	3,984	3,978	3,955	3,820	3,732
Total all dailies	16,219	16,113	16,588	15,691	15,526	15,547	15,662	15,442	15,440	15,425	14,893	14,597

SOURCE: N.B.P.I. Report No. 141, H.M.S.O. 1970, p. 29.
* From the Economist Intelligence Unit Survey.
† Second half year only.
‡ From the Audit Bureau of Circulation.

TABLE 10   NUMBER OF EMPLOYEES IN ADVERTISING INDUSTRY
(The table below shows the numbers registered by
member companies of the Institute of Practitioners of
Advertising, i.e. over 90 per cent of all advertising
agency business. *The Times*, 27 June 1967)

Employees in IPA Member Agencies

	Male	Female	Total
General Executives	3,206	253	3,459
Copywriters	632	167	799
Artists	2,710	320	3,030
Media	973	525	1,498
Marketing services	425	389	814
Public relations	267	243	510
Mechanical production	1,354	136	1,490
TV, cinema and radio production	290	110	400
Secretarial	29	2,708	2,737
Juniors under 18	467	356	823
Other staff	1,892	2,506	4,398
	12,245	7,713	19,958

The most successful newspaper advertising campaign in the year 1969/70 was
the *Sun* with a total advertising budget of £507,000 (£481,000 on television
and £26,000 on press) increasing its circulation from 1,509,000 to 1,721,000.
The *Daily Mirror* with a budget of £222,000 spent £184,000 on television,
£38,000 on press, and dropped circulation from 5,004,000 to 4,443,000.

The *Express* spent £52,000 on television, £4,000 on press, and dropped
from 3,732,000 to 3,519,000. The *Daily Mail* also lost circulation from
1,960,000 to 1,814,000 after spending £75,000 on television advertising and
£2,000 on press advertising.*

* *Guardian*, 27 April 1971.

PART II

The foregoing tables represent what I take to be a sample of the significant economic quotations. These quotations belong not so much to the total scheme of which economics is a part, but to advertising as a form of capitalist enterprise. They do not tell us a lot about the total scheme other than give us some measure of the relative importance of advertising within that scheme. The ideology of the larger scheme—the ethics of mass consumption—we have considered. I have insisted that a usable critique must keep the role of advertising as mediator and interpreter of social reality steadily in view. We shall consider in the next chapter the gap between the 'manifest' and 'latent' ideologies of advertising—the gap, that is, between the agencies' self-justification and the hidden functions of their beliefs and arguments. We need at this stage however an understanding of the actual and mythology in strictly economic arguments about advertising. We need to keep firm hold on what advertising does and does not do, and such a hold will mean discarding a good deal of conventional wisdom. A main premise of the mythology is that advertising of itself maintains an expanding market. I shall take this first.

1. *Advertising and growth*

In this assertion advertising is held to generate competition, and that competition is defined as the interplay of consumption, innovation, new investment, new forms of mass production, and so on, for ever. Now there is no doubt that a form of this cycle is the platonic ideal of capitalist economics. There is further no doubt that such rhythms sound profound echoes in the hearts of advertisers, as we shall see in Chapter Three. It is also certain that advertising *intends* the generation of these rhythms as its purpose. And its success in doing so is taken to be demonstrated by the continuance of expansion, the disappearance of slumps, and the unexamined conviction we all carry around that expansion in these circumstances is a function of a free consumer society, freely making choices and freely regulating growth rates and profit margins (and price cuts, too) in the best of all possible entrepreneurial worlds.

Perhaps a diminishing number of people still hold this innocently causal view of the connection between advertising and economic expansion. The lurching uncertainties of Britain's economic behaviour in the past decade has made it clear to most of us that the national economy, like all other parts of our lives, moves beneath the weight of our history and that history binds us to an awesome complex of trading and industrial patterns, changing which involves radical alterations in a structure which can only move very gradually. The presence or absence of advertising as a loading factor in this nervous system is barely significant, though tiny factors do affect the system. The presence of advertising is critically important in the superstructure but not, it may be said, deep down. The point is perhaps best made in the United States where Madison Avenue is noisier on its own behalf as well as that of its clients than is yet the case here. The relative economic importance of US advertising is most nakedly exposed when compared with the importance of the Pentagon, which scarcely advertises at all. Even the billings quoted in Table 2 look puny beside an expenditure of $80 billion in 1970 (or × 4,000 that of advertising) and property worth $202 billion, 39 million acres, and 4·7 million employees. It may be objected (it has been) that influence of advertising cannot be calculated by comparison with capital input. But the U.S. Department of Defense holds in its gift $40 billion worth of contracts in production in the private industrial sector, and these contracts are tendered for and won by such giant firms as General Motors, General Electric, Boeing, McDonnell-Douglas, Ling-Temco and so on.* Here is the really powerful impulse to growth: the maintenance of a war-time economy. Without this sustained and planned injection, the free-floating economy would have drifted up and down as the creation of excess and therefore stagnant capacity followed allegedly competitive investments. The naïveté is to draw a single line from advertising to market demand to increased production to high profits to new investment. This graceful circle shuts off the embarrassing loops created by stagnant capacity and dying industries—justly done to death by that uncompetitiveness which obstinately refuses to accommodate itself to the demands of modernization and which leaves great areas of a landscape derelict for the dustmen of the public sector. The circle through high profits and back is drawn in neglect of wages

* Seymour Melman, *Pentagon Capitalism: The Political Economy of War*, McGraw-Hill 1970.

and global prices and in ignorance of world politics. We have seen that the American economy moves in time to its warfare; what we need to ask is what similar controls play over the structure of British economy in order to attain a confidence and health which it has not shown and which could not in any case be brought about by advertising. Answering such a question would take us to the heart of the British economy and the British power-élite and while we can only chart the main road of that inquiry in these pages, the journey would make it clear that advertising is instrumental and not executive in the working of the structure. To make this point is to say the same thing over and over again; the function of advertising is to mediate to a mass public a special version of social reality. Advertising is the information system whose control rests in the hands of the governors of the people. The extent to which *their* wishes, the intentions of advertising, and the freely exercised choice of the rational consumer coincide, is given by a coefficient whose terms are political, historical, biochemical and social, but mostly political.

If then, advertising does not of itself ensure steady expansion, it cannot justify the second article of its faith that it encourages price competition and the invention of new products.

2. *Advertising, prices and mass production*

Expansion is the result of economic planning on behalf of this or that set of interests. Men make plans—which include advertising—on behalf of profits. Innovation is necessary because of the drive for re-investment of high profits. But these profits repay best when turnover is very rapid. Huge sales ensure this rapidity. Consequently very expensive plant is needed to produce for a mass market in which the profit margins are necessarily small. In this situation, as is clear from an analysis of the most profitable manufacturers in this country that conditions of near monopoly are the only ones which guarantee successful mass production. The classic examples are the car and petrol industries. The giant firms spend fabulous sums on marketing in order to divide the spoils between them: British Leyland versus Ford, with a specialized minority market in very expensive alternatives (Rolls-Royce, Aston Martin, Lotus, etc.). Advertising affects neither innovation nor price. Prices are fixed within the cartel or price-ring. What advertising can be said to do here is make sure there is no crisis of over-production in which prices will fall, and recession follow. Advertising tries to make sure that consumption keeps up: that what gets made, gets sold. In these conditions advertising, as one might expect, helps the accelerating momentum of capitalism to achieve itself. There is no competition except amongst the giants who can afford the sums involved and whose spending levels go up in step with their rivals. Advertising is a force towards monopoly; it ties spending patterns to those firms who can pay to stay there. Cheap innovations from smaller firms can scarcely break into the market. These strictures do not only apply to branded goods—to cars or food or clothing; they also apply to service monopolies of all kinds, such as banks, insurance firms, unit trusts, holiday agencies, building societies. Here too we find the price cartels, the war of the oligopolies, the drive to increase demand, all the old irrationalities of the manu-facturers transpire again in what at first sight look like the necessary services of the welfare industrial state. There are exceptions. The striking success of Marks and Spencers, Sainsbury's supermarkets, and Boots, has shown that a mass organization does not have to advertise, and that honest, smart and admirably cheap designing and production make decisive sense in a mass economy as well as contributing boldly to mass education. Such firms are models for a positive future as well as strengths in the present. But by and large the cant goes that adver-tising confirms the drive of capitalism towards efficiency and cheap-ness. In truth it is coming to seem that prices are a matter of tension between human greed and the Monopolies Commission and that efficiency, clean contrary to the platitudes, is a matter of ration-alized mass production by the monopolists. The real tension is not the allegedly wholesome one between inefficient firms whose products are rejected by the free consumer and good firms kept in sprightly trim by openly conducted competition. The tension of modern capitalism is between a crisis of overproduction and a crisis of stagna-tion in which lavish plant is running idle or at half-capacity. These are the poles of the seismic stop–go convulsions of the British economy, and more or less violent alternation between them reverberates across world trade. The dramatic expansion of advertising arose in response to the need of the monopolies to drain off rising incomes without affecting the structure of society. The rational and moral alternative is to turn the resources to what is needed. Even if it is hopelessly idealistic to propose these measures on a global scale, it is at least thinkable to administer them locally. Why should we not turn our colossal surplus wealth to better public services—better schools, better health, better housing? To say that these are no longer social needs is derisory. The point is that the gap between man as buyer and as human being must be kept uncrossed. The major achievement of advertising is to have created a self-fulfilling image of public welfare as drab, brown-painted and seedy, constantly diminished by the high glamour and vivid sexual satisfactions of consumer living. The image is a projection of the social and economic institutions which for imperial reasons need to keep the gap open. The mythological projection of the image is that advertising maintains free and wide choice for the consumer. Is there any truth in this claim?

3. *Advertising and information*

The hidden metaphor in many defences of advertising is rational dialogue. 'Here are these goods or services; here are their advantages; here is how, at their most attractive, no doubt, you might use them.' Such a notion is pitiful when we look hard at the actual strategies of advertising, but suppose it were true? Could we then say that advertising helps to ensure the cleanliness of the market and the sovereignty of the consumer? Is the conversion of the advertisers to honest men all that is required? If this is so, then the educator's task would be much easier: he could point to the honest advertisements as a touchstone of worth and against these frames of comparison his pupils could sort out the deceitful and scurrilous. We should have a rational market place.

We need to be clear (again) that in a specialized but endlessly dependent society we need information about commodities. We do not fail because we are too 'materialistic', but because the materials are substituted for authentic values and human connections. The lambent squirearch who gestures at working-class cars and washing machines as symptoms of materialism misses a main point. The commodities may be merely materials: means to a liberation of action once impossible or imprisoned; in which case, splendid. But the commodities may be there in response to successful advertising which offers them as symbols of health, wealth and attractiveness. Not only is the irrational and conscienceless energy of the advertising brought out by the absence of any advertising, in an economy mobilized by advertising, of welfare and public service. If what we want is information, then advertising could bring to public consciousness the presence of horrifying squalor and degradation in modern Britain—But

What else are we silent and unresponsive about? Well-grounded predictions which have in fact been made that the collapse of the National Health Service is imminent would, one might expected, have brought questions about the nature of that service to the centre of national discussions of social questions. They have not. We no longer treat welfare questions as important questions compared with questions about productivity. 'Production for what?'—the old social democratic inquiry, voiced for example by R. H. Tawney—is not heard.*

Advertising, which is held to be the voice of a civilization, the source of information for the main circuits of society, is silent about public welfare and social values, and such a silence is not innate to the medium in all industrial society. Nobody could argue that it was the consumers' *choice* to be silent about substantive social values; rather it has been the gradual choice of the governors, in and out of the elected Governments, that informed public debate about equality and social justice shall be made very difficult. Advertising reticence on such matters is not universal; Yugoslavia, Sweden, Finland, Canada and Switzerland are a pretty diverse set of Western cultures which prove the contrary. All are in many ways less wealthy than Britain, though their housekeeping is less strained. Advertising in Britain aims to eradicate rational dialogue and even though this aim is impossible the attempt is made to exclude alien kinds of information, to close the circle to subversive evidence. The machinery of marketing, the study in psychological depth, the analysis of typologies of social profiles, the extended campaigns to promote sales represent giant endeavours to reduce choice to a predictable minimum. The intention of marketing campaigns is to restrict competition and generate a largely false appearance of choice between goods on fixed prices, whether cars, clothes, insurance policies or holidays, a choice which is in reality limited to discriminating between packages or photographs of sex-kittens. The

---

* Alasdair MacIntyre, 'The Strange Death of Social Democratic England', *Listener*, 4 July 1968.

movement of consumers to and from the brands serves to keep money in circulation and to maintain the show of busy exchange. Between the monopolists even when the cut-throat is in earnest it is always clear that failure is hardly hurtful. The only ignominy is to be swallowed by the bigger pike, and even this disgrace is rarely caused by consumer rejection. It is not local consumer behaviour which threatens the giants, it is the longterm future of a world in which uncontrolled capital accumulation will finally drive the big firms back from their ruined and starving empires to fight things out in the rich home markets. Advertising can only accelerate that process in all its despairing irrationality.

4. *British industry and advertising*

British Industry is master of its own advertising, although advertising is locked so tightly in the main structures that its decisions have become executive for the press and commercial television and its leaders move to and fro across the boards of industry, banking, civil and public sectors. Indeed a main trait of British industry is that its leading managers arrange to sit at so many tables, and that so many of them are merchant bankers. Studying the boards of directors of the biggest British firms and the communications reveals the remarkable social cohesion of the firms, the high degree of interdependence, and the invincible control exerted by a fluid group of financiers who move easily from board to board and on to the Treasury and Civil Service and back without either the electorate or the shareholders knowing or, indeed, caring much about it. This easy traffic confirms the flow of state aid and capital into private industry, and makes the organization of foreign investment in England a collaborative enterprise shared by state and private financiers but administered strictly according to the rules of broking. This collaboration is the source of British industrial planning, and there is no perceptible gap between the priorities of a Labour or a Conservative government and the priorities of the Confederation of British Industries. This state of affairs is not affected by minor adjustments like the government decisions in 1970 and 1971 to eliminate regional grants, abolish the Prices and Incomes Board, and sell publicly owned businesses to private enterprise. The changes merely mean a more naked encouragement of the monopolies. The publicly owned industries, purchased with public money, are sold off for gains which are not subsequently returned to the nation for its common welfare (schools, hospitals, houses) but appear as part of an erratic current of tax concessions made to corporations and to individuals, allegedly in the encouragement of incentive and investment, certainly in the enhancing of private wealth amongst the wealthy and private poverty amongst the poor. When this random decision is allied to tight money controls, stagnation of growth, rapid inflation, the slide of real wages and the appreciation of property, it is clear at least that an economic system which has been regarded as heaven-sent is as contingent and mutable as any convention, and that as the economists might have learned from David Hume

When I cast my eye on the *known qualities* of objects, I immediately discover that the relation of cause and effect depends not in the least on *them*. When I consider their *relations*, I can find none but those of contiguity and succession; which I have already regarded as imperfect and unsatisfactory. Shall the despair of success make me assert that I am here possessed of an idea, which is not proceeded by any similar impression? This would be too strong a proof of levity and inconstancy . . .*

There are few necessary connections between economic concepts and for them to function industry and finance has had to act on the conventions as though they were true. When a particular and unprecedented crisis gets under way, as now, of course men only grudgingly relinquish their myths: they blame their historic enemies. It is clear in England and the U.S.A. that economic action has veered in arbitrary desperation through the many dimensions of choice. The only fixed point has been since the Restoration the unity of government and capital in maintaining the present constellation of wealth, power and prestige, and in facing up to any profound criticism of these as to threats of riot and disorder. This cohesion means, in turn, that the role of advertising is the result of consensus in government in both its elected and its appointed membership, and dissent is disenfranchised.

It is important to understand just how uniform the sponsors of advertising are, and how powerful their economic fortress. Then we

* *A Treatise of Human Nature*, I, 2, 'Of Probability, and of the Idea of Cause and Effect' (1739). More particularly, the devout might read Rayner, A. C. and Little, I. M., *Higgledy-Piggledy Growth Again* (Kelley, New York, 1968).

shall understand what is at stake when we criticize advertising, and how radical criticism can only be made in appraisal of the total economic situation. Such criticism will therefore be deeply subversive and we need to say this not with particular relish but in order to grasp what measures are imaginable and what are utopian. It is timely to add that a vision of utopia is a necessary part of self-respect for any man not rancid with cynicism.

It is possible to mount an analysis of British capitalism which traces its gradual settlement from the high peaks of very early twentieth-century success. Such an analysis* would be very much to the point inasmuch as advertising on a mass scale was planned and grew in response to the altering capitalist situation. But for our immediate purposes it will be enough to consider the drastic alterations in the structure of British industry since about 1960, and to relate these to the campaigns and intentions of advertising. For around 1960 the Japanese, Italian and West German economies attained a robust health of a kind which challenged the British hegemony of international trade where only the U.S.A. challenged before. At the same time, a vast upward movement of world prices for food and raw materials was beginning, and the uneasy fluctuations of the British economy between boom and deflation were exposed and lacerated at its most vulnerable points. In response to crisis, the industry defended its own interests in the following ways. First, there was a sharp rise in mergers and takeovers. Second, British companies suddenly increased their overseas expansion. Consequently, British capital was first reconcentrated and second redeployed overseas. The overseas investment was often long term and inaccessible. The absent capital at home was provided by foreign investment and, increasingly, by the state. The state contribution came first in the form of direct grants; second, in the form of tax concessions for reinvestment; third, in the form of wage freezes. Such massive governmental commitment meant that any government could only measure its success by the criteria internal to capitalism, and not socially. Planning, therefore, became the domain of the economic and financial controllers, and the success of the national industry was and is alike the interest of industrialist, Whitehall economist, and parliamentarian. Since this success depended on the throttling of state spending and a national conspiracy of silence about social welfare and values, it is no surprise that state services continue on their

* Provided by Eric Hobsbawm's *Industry and Empire*, Weidenfeld, 1967.

threadbare way, while advertising is the main generator of respect for the strengths of private enterprise half of whose *net* fixed capital formation is found by the state. And for our purposes the State defines itself as the financial controllers, in and out of Parliament. This is the context within which we may define the role of advertising and adjudicate upon the arguments about advertising in free or totalitarian societies. It issues from the institutions which capitalist prosperity has built up in Britain. These institutions are uniquely homogeneous in composition and outlook and, therefore, in advancing their interests. The difficulty is now to know precisely where those interests lie. The compromise between labour and capital in order to drive the magic roundabout of 'modernization' begins to fall apart when it is seen that in a national economic deflation with international recession likely, unemployment, low growth, high prices, are all going to expose the vulnerability of that compromise especially when capital will give little of its traditional ground away, and looks for continual concessions on the other side. The worry is then that advertising, agent of consumption, is pressing upwards the twist of wages on prices at a time when its controllers wish to contain both without there being any social controls over their production decisions or any alteration of the internal criteria by which industry shall make its profits as large as possible. Large rents have appeared in the seamless fabric of mythology. Advertising continues on the assumption that the elusively delicate equipoise of the economy is recoverable. To manage this, the controllers must find the right balance between home and foreign demand for British industry to expand with the lowest possible costs and no labour troubles. The only way this can be achieved is by encouraging profits to rise as quickly as possible, cutting public spending back very hard, and by hoping for the best in international liquidity and the expansion of world trade. If all goes well—and many of the predictions have little more status than feeling the seaweed or gazing into tea leaves—advertising will fulfil its classic role of intensifying consumption for those who can afford it and of consolidating the stratifications which make opulent show and acquisitiveness a corollary of status. But it will discharge this duty with some misgivings. For the structure of British industry interlocks rival with rival in such complex links that, as I have shown, simple competition has long disappeared, and the aim must now be to complete so scrupulous a piece of market research and to follow it with so convincing a promotion campaign that the numbers of products—or policies, or mortgages, or volume of freight tonnage space or thermal units stored—which have been put out on the counter can be sold on a sufficiently mass scale to avoid overproduction, and to ensure sufficient profits for surplus and reinvestment in next year's retooled plant. But not only this. The capture of the market must not be so successful that the distribution of profits is so violently disturbed in another sector that wage demands and price rises inconvenience the nice balance found by the first piece of marketing. When there *is* overproduction then the monoliths contract, and a recession follows in this or that sector. In order to soften the angular lines of this lurching graph, the corporations have moved defensively into protective groupings and mergers. In this new configuration, advertising takes on a new role. As well as the old competitive aims—'Drink this, not that; it'll make you more drunk'—there is now the need for the very much more general diffusion of capitalist uplift and 'image-making' (*sic*). The point here is to encourage confidence in the system, to release bromides into the air which will, the advertisers hope, bind confidence, expansiveness, and loyalty to a given group of firms, and crucially to an existing way of running them. One interesting detail hidden in the totals of advertising expenditure is the £10 million spent in 1968 on financial advertising in the big dailies and in the local press. These panels are the chairman's statements to his shareholders and his summaries of balance sheets. The corporations do not just intend these to be read by shareholders; after all, they send out copies of their annual report. The advertisements are an exercise in building confidence and they take their place beside display panels as a rite of public self-justification. One has only to read a few to know that their partiality and well-upholstered cadences prevent their being a source of disinterested public information. This secondary role of advertising becomes more and more prominent as the independence of capitalist state and big corporations hardens in its new outlines. It is my view that this role will gradually usurp the primary historical role of capturing a proportion of the market and binding it to a product. The prehistoric competitive role, to inform the public of what is available and with what attributes, has long since gone into small print in the classified section, and is institutionalized in that surrealist and wholesome weekly *Exchange and Mart*. The secondary or image-building role keeps the moral climate suitably consumptive. Its effectiveness is probably incalculable although, as we shall see, its style and value-system suffuse the whole system of communications and therefore, one may guess, the real language of men. Within this general ozone, pockets of hotter air denote the still widespread zones where the main pair or trio of rivals compete for the market (the small-scale competitor has no chance of breaking into the combat without impossibly expensive advertising campaigns unless he markets a small range of long-established or fashionably antique products). One important change is taking place in the very rich countries where manufacturers are beginning to cater intensively for specialized tastes in certain social groups. Thus, instead of marketing, say, cigarettes for everybody, the maker produces a brand with a certain type of person ('consumer-profile') in his sights. With the density of market research he has available, the maker also knows how to reach his likely purchasers, and by what appeals to make them so. He is helped in this by the increasing exclusiveness and specialization of newspapers and magazines, as well as by the remarkable increase in the amount of space and newsprint now given to the discussion of business affairs, fashion, design, and performances, an increase which itself represents an utterly unquantifiable extension of cash-values and the ethics of

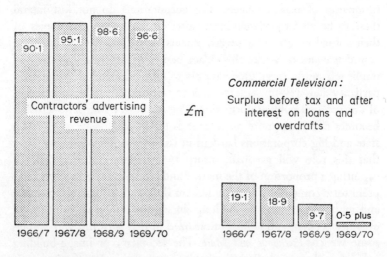

Commercial Television:

Surplus before tax and after interest on loans and overdrafts

SOURCE: *Sunday Times,* 1 March 1970.

Tell your children about the new Kellogg's Corn Flakes painting competition

2502 Giant Legoland sets (each worth over £10) must be won

If you have children under 15, tell them about the new Kellogg's Corn Flakes Painting Competition – because they could win one of the 2502 Giant Legoland sets Kellogg's are giving as prizes. Children love playing with LEGO – and this is a competition that could win them the kits to build every model in the picture!

And don't forget the younger children either, because this is a competition with *equal prizes in three age groups:* up to 7, 8 to 10, and 11 to 14.

Every child has the same chance!

So make sure Kellogg's Corn Flakes are on your shopping list.

Full competition details are on the Special Packets!

Plate 5.   Austin Morris

The perfect car for a dirty weekend.

The fact is lots of people are put off going out in bad weather because they're just not sure how their cars are going to handle.

Not so for the driver of the Austin-Morris 1300. He's confident. Confident that front-wheel-drive will "pull" him out of trouble, while others are just being "pushed" into it. He knows his car will hug the road, whether there's rain, snow, ice or mud.

Even if half the road surface gets washed away–he doesn't worry. Hydrolastic® independent suspension will take all the punishment.

And he won't.

Moreover this 1300 is up to a foot shorter than its comparable American owned competition, so it's easier to park.

And at the same time there's much more leg room in the back. And breathing space all round. We've achieved this by mounting the engine sideways. An engine by the way, that will whisk you to 50 m.p.h. in 10.6 seconds.

Which sums up the 1300, big brother to the highly successful 1100.

Take one out on the next dirty weekend. For a Test Drive.

AUSTIN-MORRIS | 1100 MK2 & 1300

Recommended price for 1100 from £770 inc. p.t. And 1300 from £823 inc. p.t. Automatic £98 extra inc. p.t.
Extra is charged for delivery, seat belts and number plates. Figures quoted from Autocar.

advertising. The decrease in the profits of commercial television registered in the table above (p. 46) may represent the effects of manufacturers' growing attention to the manipulation of more precise social groups who can be more certainly reached through their known weekly reading than through the indiscriminate broadcasting (it is the right metaphor) of TV. In 1971, with a new government, we can only speculate how the present (and typical) uncertainty and contraction will correct itself. With the putative onset of local commercial radio it seems likely that, as in the U.S.A., revival will come through much more commercial broadcasting aimed at known though smaller audiences.

We may arrive therefore at the following summary conclusions about the economic functions of advertising.

1. The annual expenditure on visible advertising is £520m in 1970 or 1·4 per cent of the Gross National Product.

2. This figure does not include the £670m spent in 1970 on packaging, some proportion of which belongs to improved hygiene and preservation.

3. The leading British advertising agencies are deeply penetrated by American ownership and capital and may expect to become more so. The involvement of American capital in British advertising is of central importance to the development of the industry.

4. There has been an immense extension of the coverage given to business, market and advertising news in all mass communication.

These are the main economic data of this review. When we come to appraise the economic effects claimed on behalf of advertising, then few of them can be upheld, none can be proved and most should be rejected as irrational or inhuman. The first claim is that advertising encourages the free competitive play of the market. We may dispute this on the grounds that the allegedly free play disappeared with the arrival of state planning, and the coincidence of private and public capital investment without social controls. Secondly, we may rejoin that advertising does not sharpen competition so much as exclude smaller competitors and therefore help to create monopolies. Thirdly, advertising in pushing up demand irrespective of national or world stability creates new capacity plant which can just as easily fall stagnant when under other pressures the market contracts.

The second claim lodges that advertising creates a mass market and mass production which in turn lowers prices ('unit-costs') and makes for innovation. Against, this, we may object that the innovations are often trivial (greater speed and baroque details instead of greater safety and less pollution in motor cars). Secondly, the mass market is dominated by oligopolies (cars, again) who fix their own prices within one ring. Goods whose prices have dropped noticeably (records, refrigerators, artificial fabrics, radios) have not all advertised extensively, and have in some cases (radios, records, tapes) been mainly affected by electronic discoveries emerging from the arms race, in others (fabrics) have been the product of the monopolies (I.C.I. and Courtaulds are certain to merge their fibre interests shortly). Advertising has made no contribution to lowering prices. Finally, if we can imagine a science-fiction discovery by a small entrepreneur which lowered prices he would be quite unable to sell it without an enormous and costly advertising campaign.

The third claim is that advertising is the indispensable source of information about goods available in a mass society. This claim can be decisively rejected by hysterical laughter and pointing at almost any TV or newspaper advertisement. If however it is claimed that advertising *could be* such a source and resource, in this event would this honest world crown the consumer sovereign? By its own logic, no. Humanly we need commodities and therefore we need to know about them. But the *point* of advertising is to encourage irreflective consumption, reinvestment of surplus in new capacity plant, and so on in perpetual motion. To say that advertising on these terms could and one day might tell rational truths is to commit a logical self-contradiction, *A* and not-*A* become equivalent.

If the classic defences of advertising dislimn under scrutiny, what solid economic achievements replace the phantoms? Well, first, advertising has so successfully penetrated the structure of British industry and the public mind that society sees it as a quite self-explanatory provider of capital for the national communications system outside the BBC. Amazingly, only a handful of people see this means of financing radio and television as at once ludicrous and threatening. For in what public interest shall a group of very rich shopkeepers select and filter international news and popular culture? The first achievement of advertising is its most incontestable. Secondly, advertising has devised a set of techniques for the analysis of social behaviour which enable manufacturers in near-monopoly and very large corporations to divide a mass market fairly evenly between them.

If one competitor does fall out, this is no example of the free play of the market finding out the weak and uncompetitive—pre-Keynes economic Darwinism. All that happens is that a merger declares itself, the shares are redistributed and the brand-names shuffled. But the undoubted correlations between advertising campaigns and rates of consumption point to the third and fourth economic achievements of advertising. These are that advertising encourages a condition of unbroken purchase and that this prodigality, so necessary to the growth of the mixed economy, in turn becomes part of a social and moral ideology which judges fulfilment in terms of private possessions and ostentatious display. Advertising concentrates attention on private wealth and spending; it empties of meaning any larger and more generous impulses. It makes the money spent on shirts or tights or beer or colour television into a lascivious pleasure and the money spent on beautiful schools or cleansing the landscape of beastliness left by private exploitation into a wretchedness. Every advertisement we see implicitly derides the culture, the physical uprightness, the dignity and social justice which make a living civilization possible. Instead we are offered and appear to accept the decisions made on our behalf by our governors that they can best decide upon the meaning and quality of our lives for us. It is, in its tiny way, a residue of hope that they use advertising so extensively to justify themselves. The self-legitimation is an attempt to give their actions decently rational and moral grounds. Let us examine some of these attempts.

THREE

The Ideology and Battle Plans of Advertising

Again, C. Wright Mills has succinctly stated the main premises and contradictions discoverable in the way men justify themselves and their actions by invoking in their defence the official values of social belief. He writes:

Those in authority attempt to justify their rule over institutions by linking it, as if it were a necessary consequence, with widely believed-in moral symbols, sacred emblems, legal formulae. These central conceptions may refer to a god or gods, the 'vote of the majority', 'the will of the people', 'the aristocracy of talent or wealth' . . . such master symbols, relevant when they are taken over privately, become the reasons and often the motives that lead persons into roles and sanction their enactment of them. If, for example, economic institutions are publicly justified in terms of them, then references to self interest may be acceptable justification for individual conduct. But, if it is felt publicly necessary to justify such institutions in terms of 'public service and trust', the old self-interest motives and reasons may lead to guilt or at least to uneasiness among capitalists. Legitimations that are publicly effective often become, in due course, effective as personal motives.*

Wright Mills, as we shall see, neatly catches the irreducible contradiction in the advertiser's claim that he is at once public servant and private broker. More generally, he gives us a lead in the analysis of social ideology, a delicate term to use. If we disencumber 'ideology' of its rather strained polemical overtones, we may define it as a system of ideas about social reality which legitimates the behaviour of a

* *The Sociological Imagination*, Oxford, 1959, pp. 36-7.

social group. What it is important to perceive, of course, is the often enormous discrepancy between the 'manifest' function of an ideology, which justifies things according to shared values, and its 'latent' function according to which it operates systematic distortions in order, say, to conserve the power or extend the wealth of a group. Thus, some small children may bully smaller ones and annex their toys and play space, and then excuse themselves to a teacher by saying that the little ones had flouted their boundaries, or had given them the toys voluntarily, or that it was in any case time to finish break. Again, in a harsher reality, the rich South African will explain the powerless and impoverished subordination of his servants by incantation about the servant's different cultural needs, or about his ineducable irresponsibility, or his affable loyalty to his master and the pleasure he takes in service. The first point to be grasped in both cases is that the defendant isn't necessarily telling lies to his listener; he is deceiving himself. In the second case it is essential to his self-esteem that he believe what he says. The second point is that in both cases the defendant appeals to an external sanction which he believes any listener will agree to; the small boy appeals to just reprisal and the school timetable, the white man to a moral respect for the claims of others, to an ideal of individual rationality, or to an archaic image of feudal devotion; indeed either may appeal to all three at once. In each case the explanation justifies the action by an appeal to shared standards. The construction of such standards in such a way as consistently to reinterpret and rearrange social reality is the construction by a social group of its ideology. There is no necessary gap between the manifest and latent functions of ideology. Our description of ourselves and our jobs may square exactly with how we want things to be and with how they are, but it is indeed a fortunate man of whom, in a mass and specialized society, this will be true, that his account of his own work is both honourable and accurate.

It is then a main road to understanding (and therefore judging) society to analyse public legitimations (the word is Max Weber's). Such analysis lies in the common ground between the study of literature and sociology; we may call it cultural studies. In its performance, we need constantly to keep in sensitive touch with the society and its many situations which speaks through the particular utterance that interests us at the time. Any utterance has its meaning insofar as it is communication from one member of society to another.

You cannot analyse a private language. To understand the ideology of advertising it is necessary to draw a line from that ideology back to the society, to set, in other words, the ideology within the structure of institutions. If it is now clear that ideology is an essential explanatory concept; if it is further clear that all social groups formulate an ideology as rational justification and that such ideology *may* need to distort social reality in order to achieve its own legitimation; if, finally, it is agreed that such ideology only has meaning as arising from a particular society and set of institutions (it can't, in other words, be anatomized in a moral laboratory) then we shall proceed to consider a group of public statements by the advertising industry which should serve to clarify and vindicate these propositions.

The Ideology of advertising

A number of national newspapers regularly publish business supplements which report on the progress of important industries: fabrics, tourism, tele-communications, steel, advertising. The spread and success of such supplements are themselves a measure of the deep penetration of the communication system by the corporations. The London *Times* published one such supplement on 14 May 1970 and it was interesting among other things for the Pirandellian publication of advertisements for advertising by some of the main agencies. This was one text:

NOT SO MUCH A DEFENCE OF ADVERTISING AS AN ATTACK ON ITS CRITICS
(By Francis Harmar-Brown of Bensons)

The fundamental case against advertising (though it is not often so well expressed), is that it helps to lower both the standards and quality of people's lives by deceiving them into wanting what can be profitably supplied (like Bingo and lead gnomes with built-in obsolescence) rather than what can be profitably consumed (like education, craftsmanship and culture).

It is not enough to point out that today's cheap cars out-perform yesterday's expensive ones. It is not enough to remind you that individual craftsmanship can never satisfy the real needs (material though they may be) of today's exploding populations, and that mass-production (in which advertising plays an essential part) is not incompatible with high quality and good design. It is certainly not enough to remark in passing that if Harold Wilson's speeches were vetted by the ITCA half of them would never have been delivered. It is not even quite enough to remember that the only way the cobbler can get another suit is to persuade the tailor to buy another pair of shoes. All these observations are helpful in their way, but they don't lead us to the heart of the problem.

Those of us with the responsibility of Improving the Quality of Life should remember that it is *people's* lives that we are talking about. And we have to decide at the outset whether we shall best achieve our high purpose by letting people work for what they want, or by making them work for what is good for them—since there is not really a middle way. Not even the most cynical advertising man could ever have contrived the irony of using the same words— Democracy and People's Government—to describe two so diametrically opposed patterns of life.

Most of this country's serious critics of advertising would claim to be democrats, and the real reason that they criticize advertising is because it exposes—more clearly than any other activity—the fundamental challenge of democracy: people don't always want what is good for them. Surprisingly often they do, but sometimes they don't, and advertising makes this crystal clear.

Advertising—which is no more and no less than persuasive communication— has served democracy well. If the critics of advertising would use it to help solve the problem it reveals, instead of attacking it for revealing the problem, advertising could serve democracy better still. It has long been the habit of government to bribe the electorate with their own money. How about persuading them with their own money for a change?

This will serve as useful introduction to the long business of self-legitimation by advertising which I synoptically review in this chapter. It is useful because it is public, brief, and innocent.

In the first sentence the writer congratulates himself on his own concision while genially deprecating his opponents in a parenthesis ('though it is not often so well expressed'). He rounds out his opening manner with a *faux bonhomme* jocundity ('lead gnomes and Bingo') which at the same time intends to imply that the opposition, those men of straw, only argues at the level of consumer trivialities against which they pit those mighty honorifics 'education' and 'culture'.

The second paragraph proceeds in its well-upholstered rhetoric ('it is not enough . . . it is not enough . . .') to assume that main article of advertising litany which I have dealt with in Chapter Two, namely that advertising *causes* cheap cars. He abandons the words 'education' and 'culture' (which he has characteristically betrayed himself by describing as 'profitably consumed' goods) while retaining the shine which has rubbed off them on to 'craftsmanship', and goes on to strike a nobly conscience-stricken posture by pointing to the 'real needs' of the world population, 'real' here being opposed to the unreal demands of those well-known non-realists, the critics of advertising who are further insulted by the clear implication that they are not alive to the 'real needs' of those incorrigibly material millions, who wish to stay materially alive. The insult of course extends also to the millions, but the writer would be, in his concerned way, profoundly shocked to be told so. The simple-hearted article of faith is repeated ('in which advertising plays an essential part'), the aside on Mr Wilson is not so much Tory as Chelsea, and the paragraph reaches its mock-weary and fair-mindedly indulgent peroration, 'It is not even quite enough ... All these observations are helpful in their way....'. In the face of such benign reasonableness, it seems merely boorish to insist in one's doctrinaire way that the critics don't at all mind the tailor swopping wardrobes with the cobbler; they do object to advertisers organizing the exchange. But let this pass, the writer is after all taking us 'to the heart of the problem'.

He takes us there with some amusingly placed capitals at the expense of solemn persons who would improve the Quality of Life and then with a sudden rush of solemnity himself hurries into italics for the critics' benefit who never see the *people* for the ideals. The advertiser is folks. He knows, too, the only two ways of running a society: let the people work for what they want, or make them work for what is good for them. What they want, of course, is shown by the sales charts. What is good for them—like a just and free medical service, common and equal education, a wholesome and lovely environment—these are the ideals the advertiser's critics would impose on people. When the copywriter lifts hands in horror at the corrupt manipulations practised on the word democracy by the critics and the politicians, we have reached the name calling part. The 'serious critics' claim to be democrats (we know they aren't, of course, because they don't like *people* having what they want); 'the fundamental challenge of democracy' is that people 'don't always want what is good for them'. 'Surprisingly often' the funny old things do, 'but sometimes they don't'. Once more we are faced with the unexamined assumption that the sales curve is the measure of the rational choice and the unsolicited desire of consumers in a free market economy;

the myth is lodged in a pre-Keynesian never-never land. It ignores cartels and price-fixing; it ignores monopoly conditions and government planning; it ignores the logic of capitalism and the clash of interests within its social system; it forgets the manipulative aspects of advertising, and its simple risibility. The piece has, finally, the effrontery to suggest that governments who bribe electors might persuade them instead, quite overlooking the payments made to the advertiser out of the money set down by the consumer for his purchase. But of course by this stage the writer must be in part aware of his own cynicism; not just in the easy sneer at politics (nothing like it for a murmur of applause in the Chamber of Commerce) but in the vapidity of the phrase 'persuasive communication'. Persuade whom? how? to what ends? what sort of communication? what sort of community?

I have analysed this statement so critically because it offers us a paradigm of the structure of beliefs which compose the ideology of advertising and, indeed, of its sponsoring system. They are, no doubt, confused and contradictory; some of them are nonsense, but it is in the nature of many social ideologies to contain many nonsenses. It is, however, important to understand that the main, interlocking premisses of this ideology subtend a decided picture of social reality which I have already described and which concentrates the three great elements of social control, power, wealth, prestige, in the few hands who have held them for a long time. The plain, blunt man's premisses, unevenly compounded of superstition, bad faith, ordinary and squalid greed, decency and fact, are these:

1. Economics is the crucial domain of social reality.
2. Capitalism means a free market economy and that is what presently obtains.
3. The consumer is a free agent and his combined decisions regulate the market.
4. Innovation, expansion, growth, surplus and reinvestment generate of themselves more consumption.
5. Renewed personal consumption is a measure of social progress and a moral good in itself.
6. Government interference hinders such progress and forces people into a docile conformism.
7. All collective action is inimical to individual welfare; public life is bad, private life is good.

8. Class distinctions are rapidly disappearing and private wealth is spread with increasing evenness; everyone is becoming a middle-class consumer quite quickly.
9. Advertising is a main instrument in the increase of these social and moral goods.

I have shown in Chapter Two how indefensible most of these beliefs are in any sufficient account of modern economics. The point is not their truth, it is their strength, and their continued rejustification by the relevant social group in order to consolidate their social importance and their salaries. The lineaments of this paradigm recur again and again, even when they are wrinkled by more sophisticated or intelligent economic argument. In *The Times Business News*, for instance, probably the most influential of its kind, we find this typical main leader under the admonitory heading, 'Advertising: the lessons of consumers' choice':

> The experiment in selling 'state' no-nonsense powders is important, for the detergent manufacturers have been constantly singled out by the critics of advertising. While it has to be conceded that the reduced-price powders have managed to hold an average market share of 20 per cent—and their availability is not necessarily contrary to the consumer interest—it would be a mistake if too much was read into the whole experiment. The plain fact is that consumers, exercising their free choice, chose in overwhelming numbers to buy the heavily promoted brands, which the manufacturers have always claimed are the more technically advanced.
>
> But a more telling pointer to consumer opinion in this particular market is the current turmoil between the main producers, because mass advertising has generated large-scale production of the more efficient* enzymatic products at attractive prices. The benefit of laboratory research has been made available to housewives because promotional spending is providing sufficient demand for lowering manufacturing costs.
>
> (5 July 1969)

We have here a developed form of the superstition and the fallacy. There is the instinctive resistance to critics of advertising—'it has to be conceded'; there is the reflex rancour towards any hint that social and rational considerations might influence profitability—'their availability is not necessarily contrary to the consumer interest'; then there is the pugnacious assertion—'the plain fact' (so there!). But it is not plain fact at all. The least the leader-writer could expect of

* The claims that these products are more efficient is rejected in detail in *Which?*, March 1970. A BMA report (July 1971) further suggests that they *are* inimical to health.

'heavily promoted brands' is that promotion would work, in which case what is the relation of heavy promotion to that 'exercise of free choice'? And of both to what 'the manufacturers have always claimed' which, after all, one would expect of them? Very remote it seems, when we learn that 'mass advertising has generated large-scale production' and has therefore provided housewives with 'the benefit of laboratory research'. The model is exquisitely complete, though odd as to its chronology. Disinterested science has improved the soap powders which housewives, after studying the extensive advertising, have volunteered to buy on such a scale that the costs come down. But the advertising did not *generate* the production; the buying did. And which came first, research or sales? And how did the housewife know about the enzymes? And how much did the prices come down? In relation to what prices for the 'no-nonsense powders', in relation to what profits? The likelier explanation is that the housewives bought the names they recognized from what was available in the supermarket, and as we have seen recognition and availability in a monopoly market are what load and bend the sales curves. The *Business News* leader is no more than a devout expression of the beliefs which have been brought to underpin advertising.

Let us proceed with charting them. I have mentioned the widespread and increasing publication of financial advertising (£10m in 1969) in the special sections of the press. It would be a major (and highly important) piece of sociology to document and analyse the content of these reports and to trace the dynasty of power revealed amongst the men who present them. The briefest glance at a group of dailies makes clear that such reports which are only read by fairly specialized parties—shareholders or investors—are consistent with the ideology. This is a truism. What we need to do is to count and heft the bulk of these reports, to understand how directly these attitudes and intentions which issue in the voices of advertising confirm and interpret the life of society.

Almost a full-page statement came out in *The Times* and the *Guardian* (3 May 1967) from Unilever during the quarrels over soap powder advertising and prices which *The Times Business News* commented on. The air of outraged virtue on the part of the Chairman is quite inimitable, especially when the Monopolies Commission asked the firms to agree to a 40 per cent reduction in selling expenses. But come, come, gentlemen,

This seemed to us, as it did to many commentators, to be carrying to an intolerable degree the assumption that bodies of this kind can dictate to industry how to run its own business. Throughout our discussions with the Board of Trade we therefore made it plain that we could NOT agree with these recommendations or with the reasoning that had led up to them, and that we would NOT agree to implement them voluntarily. In February we were invited to give an undertaking to the President of the Board of Trade to reduce forthwith the wholesale selling prices of all our soap powders, soap-flakes and synthetic powders except Square Deal Surf and we were informed that if we refused to give such an undertaking the Board of Trade would impose the price reductions by Order.

We refused to give the undertaking. We informed the President that we would challenge the validity of any such Order by all legal means open to us. We have never retreated from this position.

One can note a distinct rise in the blood-temperature of this statement. Who after all is society to exert rational controls upon the free play of private mass persuasion and price-fixing? It's hard to know whether to look injured or angry. But then, as the Chairman gingerly admits, 'public opinion might well have been critical if we had been unable or unwilling to make constructive counter-proposals', and so they agreed with the Minister to provide more powder for the same price. This settled, the Chairman can return to his minatory sternness and expression of affront:

I would be less than human if I forbore to add that the settlement, as one commentator remarked last week, 'Is a deserved defeat for the Monopolies Commission Report...'

His just anger is the stronger in that he had had no chance 'to point out to the Minister' that the Commission recommendations would be harmful not only, with the proper unction, to 'your business' (just imagine supposing that the workers might have a place in the possessive adjective) but to that supreme master-symbol 'the national interest'. Take a similar case. The Chairman of Whitbread's, Colonel W. H. Whitbread, announced:

As a result of the wage explosion, and the salary increases which must go with them, the benefits of the price award which took effect in early December 1969, will have completely disappeared by the Autumn. I cannot see how a further increase in the price of beer, which is as much needed by the retail trade as by the brewer, can be long delayed. At the same time, I believe that the highly competitive nature of our trade will keep price increases down to a minimum. We hope that the new Government will carry out its manifesto to forbear from interfering with industry and allow those who are qualified by training, ability and experience to run their concerns on proper commercial lines.

On a turnover of £200,000,000, taxation in the form of duty on beer, wines and spirits, and in Corporation Tax and Selective Employment Tax, took a total of over £78,000,000. We look forward, therefore, to seeing the Government carry out their promises to reduce taxation.*

That there was no 'wage explosion' in 1969 and that much of the taxation was paid for by drinkers and not shareholders are subsidiary to the main assumption that the social nature of industry can only be judged by 'those who are qualified by training, ability and experience' according to those well-ruled standards 'proper commercial lines'. Three days earlier the Chairman of the vast Associated British Foods said:

The inflationary conditions in this country, particularly in the latter half of the year, have made it one of the most difficult in the history of this company. Increased costs, in part due to Government legislation, have proven difficult to recover due both to Government controls and the ample evidence of growing consumer resistance to price increases in the highly competitive fields in which we operate.†

Once again governments are bogeymen and the ever-increasing profits which are the investors' dues are curtailed not only by the law but also by people's dislike of paying more (translator's note).

A review of this daily liturgy must be summary. But the shape of the ideology stands out pretty clearly; the sceptical reader can check it for himself on most days of the week in any national daily except the *Mirror*, or the *Sun*, but predominantly in *The Times*, the *Scotsman*, the *Guardian* and the *Daily Telegraph* as well the big local dailies like the *Western Mail*, the *Yorkshire Post*, the *Journal* (Newcastle) and the *Birmingham Post*. He will find, I have suggested, the simple or reductive assertions about the nature of free competition: the financial panels are after all public statements. Wright Mills's opening quotation to this chapter has emphasized that to understand the relation of ideology to legitimation and of both to the institutions of power we must note how a social group invokes the 'master symbols' of its society in its acts of self-justification. It is salutary to see what happens when the activity justified is radically at odds with some popular

* *Guardian*, 17 August 1970.
† *Guardian*, 14 August 1970.

master-symbols or magic words. Although what the author of an essay called 'The World Customer' has written is not intended for audience outside those businessmen sharing his goals and frame of reference, he exposes the tensions and contradictions at the heart of his assumptions by distorting his activities and the self-interest of his group to fit the popular magic words. Mr Ernest Dichter, President of the Institute for Motivational Research Inc., New York State, begins:

Only one Frenchman out of three brushes his teeth.

Automobiles have become a must for the self-esteem of even the lowliest postal clerk in Naples or the Bantu street cleaner in Durban.

There is a supermarket in Apia, the capital of Western Samoa (which received its independence in January of this year). I have found can openers and the cans to go with them in a remote village on the island of Upolu.

Four out of five Germans change their shirts but once a week

Amazon Indians use outboard motors in deep green water alleyways.

What do these facts and many others like them, portend for the future marketing manager? For top management in companies with foresight to capitalize on international opportunities? They mean that an understanding of cultural anthropology will be an important tool of competitive marketing. They mean that knowledge of the basic differences, as well as basic similarities, among consumers in different parts of the world will be essential. They mean that the successful marketer of the future will have to think not of a United States customer, nor even of a Western European or Atlantic community customer, but of a world customer.★

He hopes to dignify his narrowly acquisitive argument by trend-riding play with the terms 'cultural anthropology' and 'objective' in order to decide how

From objective examination of these basic cultural similarities and differences one may discern clues for serving the world customer today.

For the point of selling is to serve. This is the first appeal to one of the older master symbols. It is a particularly necessary one for the audience to accept in view of the prediction that by 1980 the 200 major international corporations, most of whom are American, will have captured over 60 per cent of total world trade and 75 per cent of its corporate assets, cf. p. 98, and in view of the present certainty that U.S. foreign investment and returns on capital combined with

★ *Harvard Business Review*, July–August 1962, pp. 113–22.

consumer technology at home has, as someone bitterly put it, 'made it easier for Basutoland to sell computers than to can oranges'. The corollary of the world supermarket run by the Titans is that the poor countries get poorer. The ideology must overlay this disagreeable fact. The 'service' itself is justified in the second stage of his argument when the mass consumption which it intends to generate is transfigured as being in itself the process of social emancipation (which as these remarks make clear is held to be an irresistible though disconcerting necessity for these brash young subordinates).

Politically, in recent years we have watched a host of new nations emerge from erstwhile colonial status. It may be argued that many colonies would have been better off staying under the protection of enlightened colonial powers. Yet their desire for independence, no matter how premature we consider it to be, is so impulsive, explosive, and uncontrollable that no other solution remains than to satisfy this emotionally, humanly understandable hunger.

In this situation to encourage wholesale purchase of mass consumption goods is to further the right sort of social change (the wrong sort has taken its unmentionable place in the communist countries).

When a South African clothing manufacturer asks how to sell more long pants to previously half-naked Bantus, he is the first one to smash the barrier of apartheid, no matter how segregationistic his views may be. The moment one starts thinking of 10 million natives as consumers, one has to concern himself with their emotions and motivations.

Research revealed a greater psychological parallel between the *emancipated* Zulu and the *emancipated* white worker than between the nonemancipated Zulu and his emancipated tribal brother. The latter is ashamed when visited by his former ethnic peers. He has learned to speak English Afrikaans, has started to wear long pants, and *often* (*sic*) owns a car—a secondhand, dilapidated car, but nevertheless a car [author's italics].

The writer gradually manipulates his terms until he is able to counterpose his concept of 'the consumer revolution' against more familiar versions of Marxist revolution and of course to endorse his as 'a revolution of the middle class' which is the clue for measuring their achievement. It is by this stage no surprise to learn that 'the most important symbol of middle class development in the world today is the automobile. It is the automobile which represents achievement and personal freedom for the middle class. And this restless middle class is the most important factor in the constructive discontent

which motivates people's desires and truly moves them forward'. In the conclusions which flow from this, however, Mr Dichter attains the apotheosis one anticipates and the automobile is transfigured from the *symbol* of desire and progress into the historical process itself. More cars means more progress. Quite quickly, of course, more consumer goods of any kind can be converted into the same equation. More of any goods means progress. It is the classical belief of capitalist ideology and it finds representatively candid expression here. It takes its place at the head of a hierarchy of beliefs whose dismal and wizened stereotypes still get about with astonishing sprightliness. Indeed it is the point of this chapter that their continued resurrection is part of the necessary ideology which gives energy to advertising. Thus in his taxonomy of nations, Mr Dichter lists the classless society like Sweden where we find 'a socialistic security and equalization which sounds (*sic*) like paradise' but which (reassuringly) 'often leads to loss of incentives'; we also find—admittedly before the days of the American resistance—a parody of the U.S.A. as 'affluent' paradigm, the conditions to which all other countries aspire and which they will eventually attain. At the moment England, along with Australia, France, Italy, South Africa and Japan, is a 'country in transition' in which, apparently, the working class though 'a nineteenth-century creation' is trying to 'break out of its bondage and join the comfortable middle class', while 'the upper class still have privileges and can afford maids, Rolls-Royces and castles' although (again reassuringly) 'their privileges are being rapidly whittled away', especially since as all the much-taxed middle class know by heart 'the white-collar worker often makes less money than the factory workers'. Of course

Cars are pampered in these countries. They are an extension of one's personality. They are given pet names. They represent major investments. Cars are outward symbols of success. There are still many first-car people, who have only now bought their first proof of 'having arrived'.

The robust philistinism of this, its blind and complacent self-righteousness prepare us for the subsequent stereotypes which among groups lumps together Cuba, China, Spain, India and Mexico as 'Revolutionary countries for whom the point of life is to 'enjoy it through the revolution in industry'. He evacuates social change of the political meanings which give it direction so that he can administer the universal bromide of mass consumption of U.S. goods. In a banal coda he clears away the last difficulty: that mass consumption does little for social justice, or liberty or equality or any noble ideal. The idea is unhealthy and anyway foreign.

Many recent stories in the press—most of them picked up in foreign countries—make it appear that we ought to be ashamed of the good life we are leading. This recanting has its origin in a deep-seated guilt feeling which is unhealthy and dangerous. Some of the recanting is directed against a number of specific products, such as electrical gadgets, big cars, luxury and leisure time, and merchandise.

The real measuring rod of the success of one system over another should be based on the happiness of the citizens, their creativeness, and their constructive discontent. The desire to grow, to improve oneself, and to enjoy life to the fullest is at least equal, if not decidedly superior, to the goal of being ahead in a missile or a satellite program.

Our present life, therefore, should be presented as a challenge to the outside world—not in a boastful way, but as a life attainable by everyone through democratic and peaceful pursuits.

Marx summarized this kind of apology a century ago when he wrote of the bourgeoisie's belief 'that the *special* conditions of its emancipation are the *general* conditions through which alone modern society can be saved and the class struggle avoided'.

The dominant tone of this revealing essay is mild, conciliatory and encouraging. It is a useful exposition of the LCM of advertising ethics and assumptions and because he empties the recitation of the thrusting and aggressive accents which were learned in the past from the robber barons, its author is usefully representative of that mild, decent and crass amnesia which is the normal social wisdom available to the voices of the free market economy. On occasions, perhaps that voice is raised more angrily. In a brief exemplary statement, Mr Enoch Powell rejected in cadenced outrage the idea of social controls on advertising:

... do not ask us to admit by implication what we deny, and to plead guilty to what we do not recognize as an offence. Unless and until the law requires otherwise, we have the same right as other citizens to conduct our affairs, and to earn our profits, as we think fit.*

By these tokens, morality is a function of law, and any profit-making goes this side the law. But then this speaker has said elsewhere,

Often when I am kneeling down in church, I think to myself how much we should thank God, the Holy Ghost, for the gift of capitalism.†

* 'Advice to Advertising', *Listener*, Vol. 82, No. 2105, 31 July 1969, p. 134.
† Quoted in T. E. Utley, *Enoch Powell: the Man and His Thinking*, London, 1968, p. 114.

It is rare, however, to find such a stark assertion of the virtues of the free market and mass consumption (it is nonetheless an important if tacit basis. The ideal-type market with the gentility removed would be very tough: repeal the Trade Disputes Act, unmake the nationalized industries and so on). The more anaesthetic air of public debate in England and the U.S.A. encourages more languid and lengthy acts of apology. Certain genteel assumptions are made about the parameters of discussion, and the conversation goes on from there. Thus the authors of *Advertising in a Free Society** whose publishers describe themselves as 'an educational trust' whose aim is 'to promote a better understanding of economic principles' and which 'derives strength from being able to . . . teach economic truths without having to adjust its thinking to political considerations' define as we might expect 'free society' as ongoing capitalism. It is rapidly clear from the book that both authors and publishers are undertaking a quite specific act of self-justification and since few people are likely to read it, its interest lies in the fact that the institution felt that it needed to sponsor such a document. It would be easy and tedious to anatomize the sillinesses of this book; the butchery would have its point, because it is symptomatic that the level of debate is so low. Perhaps this penury is inevitable with the official ideologues of any system. That the defence of capitalism need not be unctuous is shown by the swiftness, clarity and force of Keynes's fluent prose:

But, above all, individualism, if it can be purged of its defects and its abuses, is the best safeguard on personal liberty in the sense that, compared with any other system, it greatly widens the field for the exercise of personal choice. It is also the best safeguard of the variety of life which emerges precisely from this extended field of personal choice, and the loss of which is the greatest of all the losses of the totalitarian state . . .

Whilst, therefore, the enlargement of the functions of government, involved in the task of adjusting to one another the propensity to consume and the inducement to invest, would seem to a nineteenth-century publicist or to a contemporary American financier to be a terrific encroachment on individualism, I defend it, on the contrary, both as the only practicable means of avoiding the destruction of existing economic forms in their entirety and as the condition of the successful functioning of individual initiative.†

---

* By Ralph Harris and Arthur Seldon, *Institute of Economic Affairs*, 1959.

† J. M. Keynes, *The General Theory of Employment, Interest and Money*, Macmillan, 1936, p. 380.

But the ideologues are not using this vocabulary: it is noticeable that they appear ignorant of Keynes except as the source for sampler texts. All they have taken from his intellectual revolution is what, predictably, all their peers took: the idea of lavish growth as the solution to all the problems of full capacity, surplus and reinvestment. For the rest, the old phantoms walk the stage:

The main essential is that there should be freedom for suppliers (in the light of their greater knowledge of costs) to respond to the preferences of consumers (perhaps in the light of their greater knowledge of commodities). And the only certain guarantee of that freedom is a free economy in an open society.*

The bromides may be checked against the synopsis earlier. We are back in the darkest days of the cold war.

In a democracy the individual is exposed to many sources of information and persuasion. He may complain of a surfeit of advice . . . he may learn by trial and error what to accept and what to reject: but he is better off than the victims of a State monopoly in persuasion. Experience in every totalitarian country shows that even after years of indoctrination aimed at ironing out individual preferences, compulsion remains the chief instrument of government. In practice the choice is not between verbal persuasion and physical coercion. A free society relies on a great deal of the first and a minimum of the second; but a state-controlled community gets more of both, with the difference that the 'persuasion', being censored, is itself mental coercion.†

We have a free society; you have a free society; they have a totalitarian one. The book is a hornbook, a manual of daily devotions. It is notable, however, because it embodies the co-operation of interest group, moral symbolism, institutions and ideology.

Harris and Seldon are, so to speak, Moral Rearmers of the British Advertising Industry. If we turn to a more self-confident and sophisticated enterprise it is relevant to notice that there are plenty such documents to be found in American imprints, and it is possible to surmise that in the U.S.A. the collapse of liberalism which once kept up the idea of social policy in the face of the corporations and the Pentagon has already antedated its parallel collapse in Britain.‡ Yet the assurance and the nature of the conclusions which follow from

* Harris and Seldon, p. 52.
† ibid., p. 82.
‡ It is sharply to the same point that the same generalizations may be tested in the weeklies in West Germany. The much more astringent traditions of *Le Nouveau Observateur* and *Le Monde* in France critically influence the conventional rhetoric, as May 1968 showed.

the Research Professor of Economics, New York University, precisely echo what is called the consensus in Britain.*

Professor Jules Backman, writing of the U.S. economy as a spokesman for the business interest with all the armaments of scholarship at his command, concludes that:

1. Advertising contributes to economic growth and hence to an expanded number of job opportunities. The development of new and improved products has contributed to the growth of our economy.
2. The creation of mass markets through advertising may contribute to the economics of mass production. The result has been an ever-larger supply of goods at prices within the range of the consumer's pocketbook.
3. The expenditure for advertising do not represent a net cost to the economy . . . part of these funds make it possible to finance a wide selection of magazines and newspapers of all shades of opinion as well as to provide radio and television entertainment.
4. By preselling the customer, new and more economical methods of distribution have been made possible.
5. Product differentiation as reflected in brands makes it possible for the consumer to identify the manufacturer. Thus it becomes vital to establish and maintain high standards of quality which the buyer then associates with the brand.
6. Advertising provides a major source of information about old and particularly new products.†

And here, like the James Thurber cartoon, they come again, backed this time by the gigantic and mild-mannered arrogance of the American bibliographic apparatus (the book is essential reading for anyone who wants to understand the immense resources which in the U.S.A. are poured into the study of market manipulation as opposed to market supply. The human waste, institutionalized in a dozen forms from University faculties to multiple conferences and periodicals is heart-stopping in its busy magnitude). The heresy in conclusion 1 we have dealt with; that the professor should think there is a necessary causality between growth and new jobs is at this time of day incredible. Let

---

* The penetration of English Universities by Business Study Departments is limited as yet. It is no doubt a measure of my doctrinaire stubbornness that it already seems to me too far advanced. Business studies only examine forms of revisionism; they never put in question the whole economic order, or only to deride the question. There is some memorable ammunition for the argument in *Warwick University Ltd*, ed. E. P. Thompson, Penguin, 1970.

† Jules Backman, *Advertising and Competition*, New York University Press, 1967, pp. 157–9.

him visit Detroit. In conclusion, pass over the slide from the sub-junctive 'may' to the indicative 'the result has been...', and ask whether advertising has done anything about the central and insuper-able contradiction of advanced capitalism: the conflict between full employment and stable prices which no Western country has solved. As for conclusion 3, we all know that in Britain at least this is a simple untruth, though the TV companies go forward as if it were true. Here a newspaper with a one million circulation is almost bankrupted by the deliberately created economics of our press. Television is shaped by the need to capture and hold brute numbers; the commercial pressures enforce a policy of low-keyed audience hypnosis on a mass scale. 4 is only true to the hired ideologue. As the opening phrase makes clear, the conclusion is only possible for someone who is comfortably sure that the means of production and distribution shall return profits to a small number of hands. Conclusions 5 and 6 are by now too familiar a part of the available heresies to deserve much discussion. Monopoly and mass production conditions have long superannuated these chestnuts, but it may still be surprising to find that such an elaborate and technical venture as Backman's study delivers up this rank conformism. The study warns us of the future lines of self-legitimation on the part of the commercial interests which speak through advertising and underlines the thoroughness and stability with which the interests have constructed the dominant ideology. The ideology necessarily dictates the lines of marketing campaigns.

The procedures and battle plans of marketing

This is a brief section. It is a rapid attempt to describe the ways in which areas of society are organized into receptivity for new products and how the results are checked. I have said such work is a huge fraction of the Gross National Product which cannot be traced in any short-term tables of annual expenditure, and investigation of some sort would be necessary in any of the industrial societies. What we need to know is something of the way market research probes an already tightly structured market before, while and after launching the advertising campaign itself.

The classic campaign, we learn,* follows these truisms, under the initial heading 'Selection of the Media'.

1. Specification of the target.
2. Selection of appropriate medium, and sub-group (which newspapers, TV programmes etc.) within the medium.
3. Deciding upon the best size of advertisement, timing, frequency, position, etc.

The planner then puts to himself, rather after the manner of Dale Carnegie, the 'Ten Basic Queries' (Swindells).

1. What is the product or service (*sic*) to be advertised? (i.e. consumer durable, repeat-selling product, expensive luxury item or service [etc.]).
2. How is the product distributed?
3. What is the purpose of the campaign? (To establish a new market for a new type of product—impact needed, expensive; to sell a new product in an existing market; to change an old product; to remind—humorous or straight; to gain prestige; to obtain orders through the post . . .).
4. Why will people wish to buy the product or service? (because they *need* it; because it appeals to the senses; because it confers *social prestige*; to derive *entertainment*, to satisfy an *impulse*) (Swindell's italics).
5. Who needs to be reached? (age, sex, socio-economic group).
6-10. When should they be reached? How long a message, what required atmosphere, how much money available to competitors and to agent?

This pretty straightforward scheme, stripped of its jargon ('media mix', 'target specification', 'hard-sell impact') gives us the theoretic or mnemonic guide to campaign planning. It becomes less commonplace if we work back from the advertisements to the planning of a campaign and attempt to describe the planners' intentions, for only such description will answer the central question of this study: what are the social meanings of advertising?†

By this stage Swindells is able to give us 'the final pattern', and his account of planning a televised campaign offers useful anecdotal evidence. Having selected his audience (target specification) by sex, class and geography, the planner must pick his days and his time. If, therefore, he has £100,000 for his campaign (in 1966, cf. Table 8a-c, pp. 29-31) and

---

* From Anthony P. F. Swindells, *Advertising Media and Campaign Planning*, Butterworths, 1966; and Ralph Glasser, *Planned Marketing*, Business Publications, 1964.

† This is not the place to develop any account, though he will turn up again in the next chapter, but a great many advertising secrets are unlocked by the linguistic philosophy of J. L. Austin in *How To Do Things With Words*, J. O. Urmson ed., Oxford, 1962.

if the campaign is to appear at peak time and pre-peak in London, Midlands and the North only, and if 30-second spots are to be used:

	Peak Time	Pre-Peak
London	£1,300	£950
Midlands	840	675
North	1,120	850
	£3,260	£2,475

Thus it is revealed that one 30-second peak time spot in each of the selected area would cost £3,260 and one pre-peak spot in each £2,475.

Then, allowing say £5,000 for his film production costs, with his remaining £95,000 the planner can budget to spend £9,500 per week for a ten-week campaign of varying intensity at the peak and pre-peak times as well as juggling with fifteen- and seven-second showings. These adjustments are simply the outcome of crystal-gazing on the part of the planner, though he has the literature of the effects researchers (reviewed in Chapter Five) to draw upon. He can leave blank weeks in his ten week schedule so the viewer is prompted after a gap and the total campaign seems longer. He must take account of the horse-sense of advertising—cough medicines and analgesics in winter, holiday advertisements in January, men's clothing in time for a Saturday shopping outing, cold dinners in hot weather, mail orders and gardening on Saturday and Sunday, emergency copy for epidemics always ready. He must conduct follow-up research and test individual items where possible, one variable at a time.

With this last tip we come up hard against an assumption about epistemology and behaviour which is implicit in all the campaign planning. And here it is very much to the point that the methods of market research are so often the most popular methods of contemporary academic sociology. This is not simply a matter of the practical men picking up the latest tool-kit left lying about by the intellectuals, but of there being a profound similarity of ends and assumptions latent in the work of either. The Vietnamese war has violently estranged many careful-tongued American liberal academics from the social consensus although, of course, a disgracefully larger number have accepted Government paypackets in return for reorganizing the lives of the peasants. The conflict is heaving up the solid ground of their techniques and their epistemology. But the tremors have not yet touched the busy accumulation of statistical data, of interviewing and factor analysis according to which all behaviour can be classified within stable modes of society. The stability ensures that responses to advertisements can be safely charted and predicted within reliable boundaries. It is enormously useful for the market researcher that there is so complete and full an account of society provided by the sociologists which in turn produces a methodology precisely fitted to a view of individual behaviour as a function of social class, fixed and innate instincts (for sex, for possessions, for domestic love), of social regularities and settled milieux. Such a view suits market researchers very well. The sociology of sociology in a rich country provides them with their instruments. It is therefore no surprise to find B. F. Skinner, doyen of the behaviourists, cited in a gigantic reader for market researchers, whose title★ betrays much about American intellectual purchase-money.

Skinner's most attractive formulation for the marketeers reads:

As plausible connections with external variables are demonstrated in spite of that complexity [of the individual psychologies], however, the need for inner explanations is reduced. An effective scientific analysis would presumably dispense with them altogether.

That such an analysis will be simpler, more expedient, and more useful will not necessarily mean its adoption, because the older view served other than scientific functions ... certain long-admired characteristics of human behaviour seem to be neglected, and their absence is more threatening than any implication about the nature of consciousness or the existence of free will.†

Setting aside the hard-nosed conviction that anyone clinging to these 'long-admired characteristics' thereby damns himself as a caveman and a romantic, it is easy to see why these ideas and the huge pile of research which they have generated are so attractive—so expedient, as Skinner innocently remarks—to the marketing men. When Skinner says ' ... a scientific analysis shows that we react in a given way because similar actions in our past have had particular consequences' he provides the leading concept for a system of analysis whose manipulative potency was rapidly clear and whose self-congratulatory freedom from values (itself a fraud) makes the behaviourist an accessory after the nastier facts of capitalist life. As another

★ *Consumer Behaviour and the Behavioural Sciences*, Steuart Henderson Britt ed., John Wiley Inc., New York and London, 2nd impression, 1967.

† B. F. Skinner, 'Man', quoted in Britt (1967), pp. 22–3.

writer cited in this collection says, '. . . there is no use expecting all of them to respond in the same way to the same stimulus. Man is an irrational animal . . . But there is an internal logic to behaviour . . . Finally, man is describable in non-value terms'.

The same writer arrives by similar linguistic elisions and misappropriation at this triumphantly philistine reduction of human morality:

Words like 'motives' or 'needs' or 'drives' are rough synonyms for each other as well as for words like 'tensions' or 'discomforts' or 'disequilibriums'. Behaviour is thus seen as an effort to eliminate tensions by seeking goals that neutralize the causes of the tensions.*

These assumptions provide the main bearings for the construction both of a theory of consumer behaviour and for a marketing strategy. In their complacently honorific scientism and their emphasis on the accumulated studies of individuals the assumptions pose at no point any inconvenient questions about the market economy as the predetermined outcome of environmental conditions. The many contributions which the marketing men take from sociologists, anthropologists, economists build from the individual and behavioural base, and perceive society as a mere aggregate of innumerable such behaviours, some of them contradictory but all amenable to statistical sorting.

Thus:

One beer manufacturer wished to extend his market share among Negroes . . . He was advised about reaching this group by an anthropologist who was familiar with the special subculture of Negroes' caste membership on their purchasing behaviour. The ambiguity of their role has led many Negroes to be especially aware of articles that have status connotations and of whether a brand symbolizes racial progress. Examination of the manufacturer's marketing program by the anthropologist led to several recommendations for change. The manufacturer began to help in the support of several major social events related to the arts in Negro communities and to stress that the beer was a national brand with quality control procedures. He changed the content of his advertising in the directions of enhancing its status and quality connotations for Negroes.†

* Harold J. Leavitt, Professor of Industrial Administration and Psychology, Graduate School, Carnegie Institute of Technology in *Managerial Psychology* cited in Britt (1967), pp. 3 and 199.
† Cited in Britt (1967), pp. 27–8.

This corrupt and cringing little anecdote shows up both the ugly manipulations of a market economy and the hiring of academic abilities which in a better time and place would only be in the service of a solid morality. But Professor Britt's prodigal anthology gives us a measure not only of how widespread this grisly collaboration is in the States—if I can say that without transatlantic namecalling—and how vast an effort goes into market research.* Here it must be enough to suggest in a very general way and from a very few significant examples just how large an ambit is drawn by American market researchers and how detailed a map they can complete within it. They report innumerable experiments of a kind familiar in their method to many teachers, in which for example the testers report on respondents' perception of the freshness of bread as related to the quality of the wrapper† (cellophane is 'fresher' than wax) whereas another test tentatively concludes that according to attitude inventory tests and contrary to conventional wisdom make of car is *not* related to personality type, but to social mobility.† A great deal of the research is descriptive: partly grotesque stereotype ('the real high-brow . . .'),† partly a careful refutation of stereotype by reclassifying 'the Myths of Suburbia'; alternatively the research produces a careful profile by class, attitude, wage status and education, of the Scotch-drinking Negro† or the prominence given to a skin cream by the retailer in their drugstores.† But perhaps the work with the most important implications for the future developments of advertising as an effectively manipulating instrument is the series of reports, some intelligently chosen from works of classical sociology, on the flow of information through society and how this flow may be controlled by the marketeer. The careful study of 4,500 housewives and their view of 'department store imagery'‡ is trivially fanciful when placed beside the studies of group influences and communications. These render a typology of innovation—a system, that is, of the typical features which accompany innovation in social habits, in purchasing and consumption, in ideas—for example about status and possessions. The researchers very shrewdly ransack the famous work of the sociologist Paul Lazarsfeld in which he traces the lines of social

---

* Another large reader in the same series is *Marketing Communications—a Behavioural Approach to Men, Messages & Media*, Edgar Crane ed., John Wiley, New York, 1967.

† Britt, op.cit., pp. 162, 182, 232, 234, 252, 279.

‡ ibid., p. 417.

communication and the formation and change of attitudes, and revise him for their own purposes. They start out from the classical study of voting behaviour* in which he systematizes the inconspicuous and fluid patterns of leadership and local influence which are concealed not upon a hierarchical class ladder but within classes and localities upon the rosters, official and unofficial, of clubs, civic associations, PTAs, and coffee-morning gregariousness.† Nationally, they use Lazarsfeld to track the marketing leaders along 'horizontal patterns' via their age, size of family, special interests (other people tend to consult mothers of large families for any advice). His famous generalizations from his Illinois study is 'ideas often flow from air media and print to the opinion leaders and from them to the less active sections of the population' in 'the two-step flow of influence'. The marketeers have been quick to follow these novel and reorienting signposts. They have learned from Lazarsfeld and his many followers to identify the most important members of their audience. Their campaign plans have had to become more complex but they are now able to be much more precise.

There is no doubt that some of the claims made by the behaviourists and their marketing pupils are often a part, as Noam Chomsky has said 'of the desperate attempt of the social sciences to imitate the surface features of sciences that really have significant intellectual content'.‡ When we learn that we might use the equation

$$K = \frac{X_1 - X_0}{X_a - X_0}$$

to define a coefficient of persuasiveness K as the ratio of the shift produced to the shift advocated then we have started witchcraft again. No doubt quite a lot of market research is the new scholasticism, but its novel sophistication and the large stock of knowledge which it has purchased from the social sciences have been twice turned to good account. First, in providing models of human behaviour which validate the convenient ideology of competitive consumption; second, in making mass manipulation more readily measured, more penetrating, accurate and powerful.

* *The People's Choice*, Paul Lazarsfeld with Berelson and Gander, Columbia, New York, 1948.
  † The relevant pages are in Britt (1967), 281–97 and 426–49.
  ‡ Noam Chomsky, *American Power and the New Mandarins*, Chatto and Windus, Pantheon Books, 1969, p. 269.

FOUR

The Rhetoric of Advertising

Once we prompt ourselves to think hard about the everyday word 'meaning' we may get ourselves tangled in a number of different kinds of argument. There is the philosophic one about the nature of meanings: how do we know what words mean? That is to say, not how do we find out the meaning of the word 'gay'?—to which the answer might be, look it up in a dictionary—but, how do we know what the relations between language and experience are? 'What is the content of the experience of meaning? I don't know what I am supposed to say of this—if there is any sense in the above remark, it is that the two concepts are related like those of 'red' and 'blue'; and that is wrong.'* Now whatever the end of this exceptionally difficult argument, it is clear that language can only have meaning in a given context, and that—to return to our reading of advertisements—we take in their exceptionally dense meanings only by reference to the culture which produces them. If this looks like a truism (language is communication not expression) it is worth remembering that our reception of transmitted meanings is at once a sampling and filtering process and one that goes on largely in unconscious ways. It further seems likely that our neurological systems can only receive and sort a limited though still very large number of messages. It is a commonsense account of experience to say 'I forgot that; I had too much else to think about' and we similarly know and talk about our need to 'digest' new ideas and experiences, to make them our own. What effects we do not know and can only guess at are those of the now universal experience in the industrial

* Ludwig Wittgenstein, *Philosophical Investigations*, Basil Blackwell, 1953, II, ii, p. 176.

West of saturation in messages. We can make a rational guess. The constant saturation is dynamic and fluid. This is again a truism: we move through different environments which our eyes perceive in space as a mobile but dissociated continuity. Now the human brain perceives human communication in a qualitatively different way to its perception of the rest of the world. Consequently, to move through the bewildering diversity of signals from modern mass communication is to live through a series of critical disjunctures between the moving landscape and the cryptograms which require, however momentarily, delay and decoding by the observer. Insistent repetition of this sort, it is at least reasonable to fear, will create an involuntary and inarticulate passiveness. This is the most familiar of the charges made against advertising as mass persuasion. It is worth standing closer to the charge.

The most obvious characteristic of advertisements once we perceive them as acts of social communication is that you have no chance to refuse reception unless you shut your eyes. You see and hear advertisements willy-nilly, even if you go out to make tea during the natural breaks or flip over those pages very quickly or walk with your eyes down in the city. Equally, you are unable to answer the advertisements back. At the same time, the rate of exposure to this irreversible flow of unanswerable messages is so very high that a man's storage capacity is swamped and his powers of intelligent retrieval and comparison of the messages break down. A study of this kind is intended to provide on a very small scale opportunity for a more thoughtful reading of the messages. The point of using the chic vocabulary of information theory is to emphasize the continuous impact of these messages, their rapidity, and their single, uniform momentum. If we study the range and resourcefulness of modern communication systems and if we see how little access private individuals or minority groups have to issue rejoinders through that system then I think a more urgent weight presses at the back of those anxious, unfocused, remarks that 'advertisements are always trying to get at you' or 'they only want your money'. The corporation can distribute its information in the following ways:

1. Door-to-door salesmen
2. Mail orders and circulars
3. Shop display

4. Large exhibitions (Boat Show, etc.)
5. Public hoarding
6. Periodical and newspaper advertising and features
7. Television advertising
8. Commercial radio

Some of these means are extremely privileged doors of access to the mass systems. Private individuals and minority groups can rarely afford any means other than the first two. Dissenting voices raised against the main sources of power have generally to speak to a very small audience through minority publications which appear occasionally and cannot afford other than local distribution. The main point stands: the mass media group themselves into a single, powerful *system* and any analysis of its different performances must locate the individual utterance within the system. One way of making clear how closed the system is, is to perceive what accommodation does *not* exist, which is always harder than to see what does, and to imagine the alternatives.

The crux then is the systematic nature of mass communications. The social meaning of an advertisement reveals itself when we see its place in the system. The advertisements link the objects and services advertised with key social and personal values and symbols. Thus the latent appeal is not to overmaterialism but to some immanent fantasy released by the object, or some intense need validated by its possession. In a primitive culture, the sorcerer or shaman is centrally important to his tribe because he maintains an intimate relationship with the supernatural and his tribe reverences him because he provides explanatory systems where they only possess fragments of explanation. The witness of the shaman embodies in real life a diffuse mixture of ill-defined sentiments and images. His dependents vividly experience the spiritual replenishment supplied by the shaman's magic. He is therefore guardian of the tribe's spiritual coherence.* Not that the tribe is incapable of calling the shaman a fraud. But if they do, the accusation does not mean that his explanations and system are fraudulent. For he serves to incorporate hazy and unanalysed and partly conflicting ideas into a system; he holds together the scattered experiences of his tribe and offers the only way of naming inner

---

* This account of the function of the primitive shaman is summarized from Claude Lévi-Strauss, *Structural Anthropology*, Allen Lane, 1968, p. 174.

states, of giving subjective anxieties some external (and therefore less fearful) origin, and of giving shape to passions which could find no other expression. A large industrial society retains its fair share of shamans. A doctor, for example, is important to us as much as diagnostician as healer. When he can name a disease it becomes external to us and we can fight it. 'What's the matter with me?' is an anxious question. The advertiser emphatically does not command the prestige of the shaman, but his anonymous vantage in society permits him to circulate a novel magic which offers to meet the familiar pains of a particular society and history, to soften or sharpen ambition, bitterness, solitude, lust, failure, and rapacity. He provides explanations which contain each man and woman within their own feelings and prevent open seeing of a common condition. As we shall see, with often remarkable address and imaginative participation he projects himself into the meanings and satisfactions which men and women need to discover in their own situations. There is a brittle intensity and fragrance in some advertisements which is spell-binding as long as one ignores the gap between object and moral atmosphere which the advertiser intends shall not rise to consciousness. In order to see and understand these meanings we need to enter the world of an advertisement in a detail which can look ludicrous when written down, but only in this closely attentive and critical reading of concrete instances can we expect to come away with a sure grasp upon the intentions and techniques of advertisers, and upon the shared social context within which the advertisement finds its poignancy. It is a curious thing to say, but an adequately searching critique of advertisements requires us not only (as I have exhaustively underlined) to see their political and economic dynamos, but to remain keenly alive to the wide surges and currents of social feeling and action which undoubtedly find expression in the images of advertising. For the great machine cannot make something out of nothing, and while no doubt the prior directions of a social movement are themselves in part the result of half a century's mass consumption, the capturer of social needs must first identify their whereabouts and intensity. To understand the process, the dissenter must in turn understand the aspirations, pleasures, and suffering of his own people, and know them sympathetically from within. In Arthur Miller's great play, *Death of a Salesman*, the salesman's wife, Linda, makes this moving appeal for our pity and wonder at a human being bent

If her family starts in on you,
tell them you expect to have £50,000.

Not all at once of course. But you're young and looking to the future so you can see all the money and rises that lie ahead. If you're earning £20 a week or more, you'll have made at least £50,000 or so, by the time you're ready to retire. That's a lot of money and it'll take some handling.

We'd like to help because you're the kind of customer we want. We'll give you a cheque book (which is part of having a current account). This way your money

is safe in the bank. We look after it for you, and your life is made easier by not having to carry lots of loose cash around. With a cheque book you know just where your money goes, and we send you statements as often as you want them.

With £50,000 coming your way, we'd like you to know about our services. You're a very important customer.

Our services are all set out in a book. You can get it at your local branch of Barclays or you can send in the coupon.

BARCLAYS CHEQUE ACCOUNTS

– one of our ways to help you manage money better.

and broken by the terrible machinery of the market. Derision at the spells and charms of the advertising pedlar isn't enough; there needs also to be a living sense of what meanings the salesman can know in his life.

LINDA: . . . I don't say he's a great man. Willy Loman never made a lot of money. His name was never in the paper. He's not the finest character that ever lived. But he's a human being, and a terrible thing is happening to him. So attention must be paid. He's not to be allowed to fall into his grave like an old dog. Attention, attention must be finally paid to such a person. You called him crazy.

BIFF: I didn't mean——

LINDA: No, a lot of people think he's lost his—balance. But you don't have to be very smart to know what his trouble is. The man is exhausted.

HAPPY: Sure!

LINDA: A small man can be just as exhausted as a great man. He works for a company thirty-six years this March, opens up unheard-of territories to their trademark, and now in his old age they take his salary away.

HAPPY (*indignantly*): I didn't know that, Mom.

LINDA: You never asked, my dear! Now that you get your spending money someplace else you don't trouble your mind with him.

HAPPY: But I gave you money last——

LINDA: Christmas-time, fifty dollars! To fix the hot water it cost ninety-seven fifty! For five weeks he's been on straight commision, like a beginner, an unknown.

BIFF: Those ungrateful bastards!

LINDA: Are they any worse than his sons? When he brought them business, when he was young, they were glad to see him. But now his old friends, the old buyers that loved him so and always found some order to hand him in a pinch—they're all dead, retired. He used to be able to make six, seven calls a day in Boston. Now he takes his valises out of the car and puts them back and takes them out again and he's exhausted. Instead of walking he talks now. He drives seven hundred miles, and when he gets there no one knows him any more, no one welcomes him. And what goes through a man's mind, driving seven hundred miles home without having earned a cent? Why shouldn't he talk to himself? Why? When he has to go to Charley and borrow fifty dollars a week and pretend to me that it's his pay? How long can that go on? How long? You see what I'm sitting here and waiting for? And you tell me he has no character? The man who never worked a day but for your benefit? When does he get the medal for that? Is this his reward—to turn around at the age of sixty-three and find his sons, who he loved better than his life, one a philandering bum——

HAPPY: Mom!

LINDA: That's all you are, my baby! (*To Biff*) And you! What happened to

the love you had for him? You were such pals! How you used to talk to
him on the 'phone every night! How lonely he was till he could come home
to you!

(Act 1)

We must study the meanings of advertisements both as the projections of individuals and as the symptoms of those general patterns
which compose a culture.* What is more, close study seems the only
way of recognizing and countering that process of unnoticed saturation I have described. This is the only way to find out what is
going on. We shall take a number of different headings in an attempt
to draw the contours of the system from the concrete analyses.

Historical changes in advertising since 1930

Looking at oldish advertisements (and 'old' here means a very brief
span—say forty years) in 1972 one is immediately struck by the ease
with which they date themselves. They display an innocence and
transparency in their vulgar designs upon trivial feeling which is
obvious not because they give off a nostalgic flavour but because it
is clear that techniques of mass persuasion were so much less subtle
—less poisonous—then. The snobbery of this advertisement is laugh-
able because it is so obvious; the devices are abundantly at work
today but in an altogether more coercive rhetoric.

The CHESTER SPAT
approves
of the man
... who can read a winelist and know that Rudesheimer means Rhenish—
but is also aware that bread-and-cheese and beer makes a satisfactory meal ...
Who knows that Claret is best with an early pheasant and Burgundy with a
late—but finds coffee-stall coffee at two in the morning superb with a sav-
eloy ... Who goes to the Grand Opera because he likes music—and not
because it is grand ...

---

* Cf. Jack D. Douglas, *The Social Meanings of Suicide*, Princeton 1967: 'Almost all ...
sociological works have apparently assumed that there are no particular problems
involved in specifying what the meanings of things are to the social actors or they have
been concerned only with the "general", "abstract", "average", "patterned", etc.
meanings ... and have not attempted to show how it is that one would infer cultural
patterns of meanings from the particular, concrete, observable phenomena ...' p. 239.

Who can have his flat furnished by Djo-Bourgeois, without thinking Sheraton dull—and appreciate a Matisse while still admiring Michelangelo . . . who will wear his spats as a matter of course—neither looking as if he were off to a wedding nor coming back from a funeral. In a way a spat is meant to be worn—as naturally as a smile.*

Ten years later on a slightly different tack we find:

MARVELLOUS SUBSTANCE BRINGS BACK AMAZING YOUTH
Wrinkles are not caused by age but by lack of sufficient biocel in the skin to keep the tissues firm and plump. Prof. Dr Stejskal of the University of Vienna has discovered a remarkable process by which biocel can be extracted from young animals and applied externally. By the use of this remarkable product wrinkles on women from 55 to 72 years of age disappear in six weeks' time.†

Here again it is the ponderous verbosity and obviousness we first notice. No doubt our quickness is due partly to another generation of living with advertising and learning its tricks, but advertising itself has changed under the impact of electronic invention and behavioural psychology. It still makes the same appeals to magicians (Dr Stejskal), to black magic (biocel), to our fear of decay (women from 55 to 72) and need for an admiration which we think will disappear as we grow old; but the appeals are now in much more muscular training than this lumpy slogan.

These two advertisements, though accompanied by small hand-drawn illustrations, are principally verbal. The signal change in advertisements since commercial TV gathered transatlantic pace has been that they have become visual, and reading them involves as much perception of the way image relates to brand-name and to text as it does decoding a verbal message line by line. Plates 1 and 2 mark the stage reached by 1950. The pictures still look dated, but their organization has come on a long way. The placing of the text around the stylized bulges of the girl in Plate 2‡ makes the girl the main statement of the advertisement. The tumbling hair, the gleaming thighs and bust (and Agamemnon dead) are now vastly familiar in more overpowering presentation as we shall see, but even here they give off sufficient erotic voltage. The point is made if here and in one or two later advertisements we compare the lines of the girls'

* Quoted in F. R. Leavis and Denys Thompson, *Culture and Environment*, Chatto and Windus, 1933, p. 15.
† Quoted in Denys Thompson, *Voice of Civilization*, Frederick Muller, 1943, p. 86.
‡ Cited in Marshall McLuhan, *The Mechanical Bride*, Vanguard, N.Y., 1951, p. 79.

bodies with the bright young thing in the comic postcard (Plate 3).
As George Orwell says, the postcard drawing 'lifts the lid off a very
widespread repression, natural enough in a country whose women
when young tend to be slim to the point of skimpiness',* but is at
the same time a jovial satire on the Englishman's private fantasies
about 'voluptuous' women which derides those fantasies as the
adolescent nonsense they turn out to be when checked against the
realities of a human body. The bodies in the advertisements are
undoubtedly lubricious even on a casual glance. The 1950 girl comes
fairly early in a line, and it is clear that the copywriter is a little abashed
in her company. The slightly old-fashioned slang 'wows' the arch
use of 'the ladies', the suggestion of 'father's day' further down all
lend the bathing belle accents of respectability and harmless suburban
flirtatiousness. But the disposition of space, the reduction in words,
the visual shock in this example are prophetic. Plate 1 is in many
ways a dinosaur. The appeal to hollow goals of success and failure,
the comforting implication that the thrifty, provident home-lover is
the better man, the tweak at people's fear of the future, the sham
statistics, these are all familiar enough. But the clumsy obscurity of
the firm's name, the blocks of print, the listless sentences and glum
drawings all seem almost endearingly ineffective now that the advertisers have learned so much from the psychologists, the market
researchers and even the film directors whom they copy or hire.†
Let us turn to the situation in 1970.

The modern rhetoric

In his admirably crisp review of the functions and techniques of
advertising, Stuart Hall says,

* George Orwell, 'The Art of Donald McGill', *Critical Essays*, Secker & Warburg,
1946, pp. 104–5.

† E.g. 'I tried the same kind of shot Antonioni used in *L'Avventura*.' This was a random
remark over-heard today at a display of films by their makers and was a measure of how
hard Film Contracts, Limited, was trying to prove its point that art can lie behind the
best of the 'commercials'. Karel Reisz's work for 'Persil', Joseph Losey's for 'Nimble
Bread', Anthony Simmons's for 'Shell'—these "demonstration reels" were presented
as if they were to film advertising what the works of Griffiths were to film features. The
Company may have been telling me tales in the politest way, but it did successfully
demonstrate that some of our most promising film makers can experiment with technique
in the 'commercial form'. The *Guardian*.

The advertiser, then, must turn to other areas where we are more vulnerable, and make his appeal either in terms of the established human meanings and values which have validated in our own experience or culture, or to those social and human aspirations which are not adequately expressed or fulfilled in modern life.*

He goes on, following *Culture and Environment* and *Voice of Civilization*, to classify advertisements by degree of technical elaboration along a scale from simple to sophisticated and then by the kind of appeal made to the reader, this time grouping them in 'clusters' of appeal to snobbery and social ambition, to 'glamour and luxury', and to 'dreaming and fantasy'. As he implies, there are many different axes along which we may classify advertisements, and we can devise such a general typology or system of typical features only by studying very large numbers of advertisements in different media and different publications. It is also important in developing an adequate critique of advertising that dissenters are reasonably consistent. We squander an important effort on behalf of human reason if we do not build on past work of this kind—there is in all conscience little enough of it when you heft the enemy's labours. I shall therefore start out from Hall's and the earlier categories, and attempt to expand them.

Stage 1. Simple

GOAL
GETTERS

Two great styles from the Simlam range of football boots. For men and boys. Built by experts to give players top-class form. Always!

For Simlam boots are supple and light. Marvellous for maintaining the tightest ball control.

Wear 'em and your skill will really shine. Slicing through defences with wings on your feet. Cracking home goals with a power and punch you've rarely known.

Yes, Simlam guys are straight shooting types.

Time and again!†

* Stuart Hall and Paddy Whannel, *The Popular Arts*, Hutchinson, 1964, p. 319.
† *Goal*, 29 August 1970.

There is little complication here. The advertisement appears in a special interest magazine and confines itself to general exhortation to buy (together with the now universal transference of human attributes and skills to the possession of objects; i.e. possession of the magic object confers the skill) and technical details about the boots.

BEST AUTUMN BONUS for your Garden!

Give your soil a break. Give it an Autumn application of natural Cutting's Compost. Specially prepared from selected Stable and Farm manures. Cutting's Compost is an all-beneficial balance of nitrogen, phosphorus, potash, trace elements and humus. There's no waste! It's clean, odourless, easy to handle—and economical! One bag dresses 540 sq. ft. Any left over can be stored indefinitely, indoors or out . . . in its convenient polythene bag. Use Cutting's Compost for: General Garden Manure; Top Dressing; Making Potting Soil; Making Seed Box Compost. Plants thrive on it! Detailed instructions are included with your order.

Special prices for Horticultural and Allotment Societies, etc., on application.

ORDER YOURS NOW!
Before prices increase due Sept. 16th.*

This, too, is indistinguishable from similar panels in pre-war gardening magazines: technical information, plenty of words, a rather manic use of exclamation marks, and then the reference to prices, which have disappeared in the nebulous imagery of mass advertising. Not surprisingly, it is the hobby, special interest, and technical magazines which contain most such advertisements, and this is reassuring. The enormous variety of such magazines which can be checked on the counters of any large-town newsagents, bears witness to the diversity and individualism of people's private lives in this country. The annual renewal of over two million fishing licences, the enormous circulation of the practical householding, decorating, carpentry, and metalwork magazines (adding up to nearly seven million), the significant *complaints* from the garage owner's associations that too many private motorists are maintaining their own cars, are only the most obvious examples of the tremendous busyness of people's private lives. Any stranger looking out of the window on a railway journey is likely to notice the ubiquity of the small garden, perhaps the most densely productive agricultural land in the world

* *Amateur Gardener*, 5 September 1970.

and, along with football, the most certainly shared and common area of British culture today. New neighbours make their first, tentative contacts in talking about their vedge or their roses; old men maintain long friendships whose depth no outsider could measure from their slow, broken ruminations about the state of their petunias or their dwarf french beans. I emphasize this human activity because it is the best-known example of an enormous range of private activities all of which take people to consult the journals, read the advertisements, buy and use the goods. The cycle revolves under the energy of enthusiasm and careful information. On the whole those who practise the hobbies know a lot about pigeons, or dressmaking, or making model aircraft, or cross-country running, or photography. Consequently their relationship with suppliers is straightforward and confident: they are well able to relate their purchases to the relative significance of their hobby in their own lives, and their decisions about their purchases require and receive (except, as we say, for the 'fanatic' pigeon-fancier or rose-grower) a sane and sure evaluation of the claims of cost, need, value, and use. Because there is a straight understanding of the activity, I think we find in the rich and busy area of private life some of the best parts of our culture. And the suppliers fill the diagrammatic or platonic function of suppliers in the capitalist market: they respond to demand, they provide information, and in a modest way, they compete as to prices. On the whole, the suppliers in *Amateur Gardener* look on their customers as 'users' and not 'consumers'—a crucial distinction. They probably remain in this early capitalist idyll for two connected reasons. First, the suppliers are mostly small local businesses which can remain content in the present scheme of things with a low absolute rate of growth; second, the specific gravity of all these private pastimes is their privateness. At a time of unique moral and social confusion, people are probably most sure of what we may call the family virtues—that low-keyed domesticity, emptied of a sense of history and a sense of destiny, for which not charity nor compassion but a rather tired, washed-out mixture of these, thoroughly decent and honoured as 'kindness' is the primary virtue. The family virtues beget family pastimes and hobbies. On the whole they do not produce a strenuous passion for individual endeavour, nor a sense of common effort or concerted aspiration beyond the neighbourhood. It is, however, beyond the neighbourhood that the critical confusions arise, and it is in these realms that men and women become consumers and the new techniques of advertising come into play. The special interests and hobbies, their magazines and TV programmes, the societies, conversations and friendships which they engender, remain as a model—a simple or complicated pattern of living in which men and women find freedom and satisfaction, explore and know a part of their lives as their own.

Stage 2. The 'compound'

At this point on the scale the simple giving of information accompanied by modest encouragement modulates into fuller orchestration. It is here that atmospheric harmonies begin to invade the illustration of the object and here, too, that we begin to study the major source of advertising change since about 1960: televised advertising. In spite of the distinct movement away from advertising on television (Table 3) towards the more precisely measurable audiences of particular newspapers and periodicals, the movement has taken with it the skills learned from filming especially under the heavy pressure which reduced the conventional time for the natural breaks from a sequence of one minute to a sequence of fifteen-second spots, a concentration which clearly required more and more innovations in visual shocks, memorable slogans and brand-names, brief but catchy jingles and violent kinaesthesia.

The first version of the compound advertisement is perhaps the cut-price panel of the kind which fills local papers and the backs of cereal packets (Plate 4). It is no doubt a guileless document, although there is a spurious smell about the collusion of cornflakes and toy bricks in the promotion of children's painting. This competition takes its place as a foray in a long assault upon parental affections and hopes, and in this case picks up the now widespread educational interest in the fostering of children's art and constructive play, and uses this prestige at a time when education has become (as must be so in a heterodox culture) a powerful but cloudy master-symbol. The prestige is there to emphasize between the lines the progressivist tip 'make sure Kellogg's cornflakes are on your shopping list'. The tone of the instructions underneath catches perfectly the eager, rather loud and breathy italics of the girlish, friendly voice in the fifteen-second spot—'And don't forget . . . Every child has the same chance! . . . so make sure . . . Full details . . . on the special packets!' If the manufacturers claim in their defence that they are the new patrons in our time of the creative life, then well and good; we know where we are. But it isn't hard to classify the cut-price or prize-winning promotion. There are plenty of examples of an even simpler sort every week when, if the time of the year is right, the gas boards will release half-page spreads and fifteen-second films of pretty children playing quietly and winsomely beside the gas fire which if you take action in time ('offer ends 17 October 1970') you can buy for £3 less than the list price. At the same time local department stores will take two or three full columns with a few drawings and a list of half-a-dozen or more 'fantastic bargains!' of 'unbeatable value!' and 'unrepeatable offers!' This candid huckstering, touched up with a little atmospherics, poses no problem to the intelligence beyond the question, why aren't the goods always that price? The answer, as the companies in question would protest, is not as easy as it sounds. They eliminate their profits on one range of goods in order to entice customers into the shop to buy others; or they reduce the price to get a new line going; or they are clearing old stock. And so on. But there still needs to be a hard-nosed response to these excuses. Our buying habits for a hundred years or so have excluded the notion of barter. We therefore come to regard the price ticket and the catalogue as speaking with a fixed authority. When we find 'slashing reductions' especially during the seasonal ritual of The Sale, we tend to feel in some surreptitious deal with the shop against the remote power which first fixed the price, and that we must take immediate advantage of this chance before all is discovered. But as the Monopolies Commission inquiry established, and the Trade Descriptions Act of 1967 began to control, a number of big stores were telling simple lies on their sale tickets. The higher price with a red line through it and the lower price underneath were in many cases invented, and the unrepeatable bargains were words for the wind which are blown where it lists in the New Year, Spring and Autumn, and clears away the old stock in preparation for the new. These thrice-yearly stimulants to the sales habits of the public are an important part of the clothing and fabric industry whose costs to buyers are probably incalculable and certainly secret. The small advertisements for mail orders which (as we have noted already) tend to appear on Saturdays in the big national dailies as well as the *Radio Times* or *Weekend* are of a piece with these stage two advertisements. They combine cut-price appeals with archaic and tiny drawings and the rhetoric of the Connecticut Yankee to match. Here we find the unadorned transfer of qualities of heart and spirit to the possession of objects—'Be as tempestuous and carefree as any Romany in our Gipsy Blouse, A bewitching see-through nylon blouse with a dramatic low gathered neckline' (*Weekend*); the naive appeal to conquer physical slightness and the diffidence that might go with it by bodybuilding exercises:

Q. Can Bullworker training even develop bodies which are weak and skinny, or fat and flabby?

A. Definitely! It's been proved by thousands of men of every shape, size and age all over the world. Bullworker training transforms weak, thin arms into rippling, muscular pillars of strength. Builds broad, powerful shoulders. Turns flat, shallow chests into deep, manly ones. Forges loose stomach flab into steel-hard, well-defined muscle. Builds that 'V' shape of a real athlete. It develops sturdy, contoured thighs and calves: changes your whole body with new energy and go-power ... And all this in record time!

What's more, I've known skinny, shy fellows who, after just a few short weeks with Bullworker, turned into real go-getters ... every inch a man ... bowling girls over with their dynamism, confidence and new found power! You really have to see the remarkable effects of Bullworker for yourself to believe them! (*Weekend*)

It speaks sadly for itself. Remember Jay Gatsby? His SCHEDULE read: 'Rise from bed 6.0 a.m. Dumbbell exercise and wall-scaling 6.15–6.30 a.m.' etc. For ...

his heart was in constant, turbulent riot. The most grotesque and fantastic conceits haunted him in his bed at night. A universe of ineffable gaudiness spun itself out in his brain ... these reveries ... were a satisfactory hint of the unreality and reality, a promise that the rock of the world was founded securely on a fairy's wing.*

These are the first examples of the second stage which Hall calls 'compound', that is, a recognizable mixture of huckstering, convenient information, the incitement to spend and a rather generalized promise of well-being and other rewards. The important act of classification

---

* F. Scott Fitzgerald, *The Great Gatsby*, Scribner, N.Y., 1925, p. 100.

is to locate such advertisement *structurally*. That is to say, what is the place of such advertisements within the total structure of advertising whose concepts of knowledge and whose symbols and imagery work to close the circle of consciousness to rational alternatives. The fantasy system works always to confirm the forms of satisfaction and fulfilment available in the present consumer market. This proposition gives us two other dimensions within which to place and understand advertisements: first, their appeal either to meanings and values which we all share and which the advertisement purports to satisfy by offering the goods linked to the meanings; we find the second dimension in those advertisements which offer this time to meet aspirations and hopes which we can *not* fulfil in our culture, by the provision of goods arbitrarily tied to values. These two dimensions hold right along the scale of advertisements except for the simplest ones which provide goods for understood uses. The two are complementary and fit smoothly together, often within the same panel or commercial. The only wedge which can be driven between them is a laborious rationalism which humourlessly attempts to see what the claims and implications are. The tight articulation and interlocking of the appeals and their symbols—the ideas and values carried in the language and images—aim to keep the system closed, and to consolidate it on its own terms. Thus, it appears to say: 'This pleasurable experience—going to a pub—is not so much a matter of easy, unforced friendliness and quenching your thirst; it is an amalgam of this beer, these clothes, this high-flying jetsetting life-style'. Or again, 'Your painful need for love and warmth is more a matter of needing to be sexually attractive, and being sexually attractive is the immediate result of wearing this amalgam of cosmetics, hair-styles and new fashions.' These two descriptions of individual behaviour leave no place for a reply which rejects the terms and demands other arrangements—here, a different social place for women, say, which makes less of sexuality and provides other forms of realization; there, less strained and chintzy ideas about visiting pubs.

The stage 2 advertisements appear at the most recognizable corners of the structure. They insist on the fundamental dynamic. Buy, they say, and keep buying; for unless you buy, use (consume), throw away and buy again, the machine stops.

Consider the familiar sort of colour advertisement which appears in every number of *TV Times* or *Woman's Own* or the *Daily Telegraph* and weekend supplements. There is no price-reduction. There are the details of the stage 2 advertisement—a recognizable picture of the commodity, a modest amount of atmospheric loading, a brand name and a blurb. What makes such examples so significant is their clear derivation from the TV commercial which I have argued is now the decisive source of ideas and what the agencies call 'creativity'. They are commercial films stood still. The colour photography is always vivid; often a reduced image set in a frame of that intense glossy black which has become a regular metaphor of extreme expensiveness in marketing, (e.g. the 'new' Players cigarette which comes in a packet of such patent black gloss as to suggest obsidian floors or table tops). In such photographs the main subject is thrown into unreally clear magnification and the background left deliberately blurred so as to hint at its pleasures without specifying them and to imply that the sensuous pleasure of this branded product in any case contains them. Such imagery is not limited to (in the grisly cant) consumer goods, and a main development of advertising in its recent history has been the conversion of 'invisible' products like banking, broking, selling air travel or insurance policies, into the voluptuous or funny or touching images of more tangible purchases. I look at some examples later. For now, consider this blurb for a soft drink:

THE MOST NATURAL TASTE UNDER THE SUN

Wouldn't it be nice to drink your Britvic where the fruit grows. Glorious sunshine ripening plump juicy fruit. Golden oranges glistening in the warmth of the sun. Fresh-squeezed to surrender all that goodness. Spoil yourself. Drink Britvic and enjoy the most natural taste under the sun. Insist on Britvic—there's no substitute for the best fruit juice.

Orange Grapefruit Pineapple Tomato Apricot

No one solemnly reads such stuff through, just as no one listens to the yearning susurrations of the natural breaks, but the assumption made is that the sweet vociferous hammers will penetrate all minds and spirits in the end. The argument is certainly strong that these rhythms have for a season penetrated and demoralized the language. Quite without careful reading or listening, the involuntarily scanning eye or ear picks out echoes of the tone and language of the TV voice, the analgesic homogenized spread of words over the subject which is at the same time the experience—'glorious sunshine', 'golden oranges glistening', 'fresh squeezed', 'spoil yourself'. It is like a debased and emasculated version of Keats's *To Autumn*:

To bend with apples the moss'd cottage-trees;
And fill all fruit with ripeness to the core;
To swell the gourd and plump the hazel shells
With a sweet kernel . . .

But it has none of its braced alertness, its strong sense of life. The cadences are a part of the sort of picture I describe and illustrate. Time and again such pictures play off the unbelievably strong images we all carry about of the ampleness of nature, its sacraments and purity, against the reality of an often poisoned suburbia.* So language and photography are idealized. The technology of reproduction throws a strong, glamorous patina of unreality across the images. No fruit salad, no lush green grove, no ice-cold stream, no cut-glass goblet, no peach-bloom cheek is that perfect. They lie at a remove from ordinary textures on the way towards the stylizations of mass consumer art. It seems to me worth adding that that art—pop painting—is itself a deeply ambivalent expression of distaste for deep-frozen chainstore overfeeding overcome by fascination with the colourful vulgarity, the machine-tooled curves and right angles. In a small way, pop art does its bit to destroy such human and moral meanings as remain in the supermarket-place.

Stage 3. The complex or atmospheric advertisement

The same techniques as in the Stage 2 advertisements appear in many of the cigarette advertisements (Plate 6).† All the potent magic of capitalist folklore—of fabulous treasures lost at sea, of the irresistible power of gold—breathes outwards from the photograph. The fairy tales of Western culture since the late middle ages, when the soldier and his tinder box, Dick Whittington, and Cinderella emerged as folk heroes from the collapse of feudalism, have filled the heart of their mysteries with fabulous caskets of gold. It seems further likely that the peculiar magnetism which charges tales of treasure lying on the sea bed, connects with the significance the depths of the ocean have in older mytho-logy and in the unconscious imaginings of all men. In these fantasies,

---

* Mary Douglas's remarkable book *Purity and Danger* (Routledge 1966) is a telling guide to the hierarchies of cleanliness and pollution which are ransacked and distorted by the marketeers ardent to attach price-tags to every stage of our culture.
† *Evening Standard*, 20 April 1971.

the ocean depths recur time and again as the vast and encompassing source of all the most intense longings of humanity. In our time there is a pointed irony in linking the major symbol of our culture, the dull, dead metal piled to the ceiling in the most up-to-date bomb-proof vaults of Fort Knox, Paris, Zurich and Threadneedle Street, with a fancy box of white nicotine tubes whose only value to the smoker is deadly but whose value to manufacturer and state revenue is in this country alone the takings from 100,000 premature corpses per year.* That the poet of this macabre conjunction is paid to be the image-maker of capitalism seems only right.

Cigarette marketing, packaging and advertising offer a central topic for any study of advertising. Not only are cigarettes utterly expendable and very dangerous, they are dirty, smelly, and unsightly. Conse-quently a great deal of advertising goes in for fresh, wholesome scenery. The associations of this picture (setting aside the subconscious and the economic ones) are clean and uncontaminated. Whatever the reality of offshore sewage, the sea is poetically bracing and salty. Similarly in the famous and very successful series of a few years ago, 'People Love Players' and the recent Consulate series set beside Alpine streams, there were clear links made between swinging young love, leafy glades, ice-cold streams and the clean, rather architectural lines of smart white packets or—as in this case—expensively gold or shiny patent black ones. Such advertisements deploy all the techniques of dreamily unfocused land- or seascapes peopled by an unforgettable hyacinth girl, 'Her hair over her arms and her arms full of flowers', and the faultless profile and tight-fitting pink shirt of her escort, all in an effort to counter the detritus of smoking, the smell, the droppings, the poison, the crumpled wrappers. In a final apotheosis Benson and Hedges (and other firms since) have doubled their symbolic money by including bonus tickets got up in order to borrow from the unimpeach-able integrity of Big Five bank cards.

Plate 7 moves a whole range of complex associations into a recognizable world. With sudden relief we might respond to this as a credible world. But it will not do to take the plain man's line and find no harm here. There is a fetching accuracy of observation: smart (but not too smart) living—polyurethene floor, dressed salad, plain oak table; the tug at the heartstrings—hands held below the table, the expressions on the faces, the matey tone 'If her family

* Henry Miller, *Listener*, 14 January 1971, p. 49.

starts in on you' as one who with knowing indulgence can tell the young man what is what. The picture hits even the most worldly-wise and disenchanted in the stomach, for it brings together a potent nexus of cash-values, possessions, security, ambition, family unity and young love. Like so much of the best TV serial acting it imparts to very familiar, ordinary behaviour a curious glamour; the acting of ordinariness is what makes a popular serial like *Softly, Softly* so successful a recruiting aid. For somehow the cups of tea the characters are drinking when Barlow bears down on them are more exciting and magical cups of tea than all the others we drink ourselves. The same here. Furthermore, the consistent exploitation of 'human angles' in news reporting as well as the medium itself make this kind of photograph (and there are more and more in advertising) immediately fascinating. What moments of other people's conversations do *not* seem fascinating to an intruder? There is indeed a distasteful invasion of our intimacy here. Not, obviously, of the people in the picture (actors, presumably) but an implied violation of all our privacies, in that this sort of private discussion is used as a net in which to trap together personal difficulties and marginal choices about which banks to use. The old parodies of the happy family all together in a drawing are replaced by the realities of this picture; 'isn't this a change for the better?'. I think not. The privacies are put on immodest show and the realities—the banker, the sentimentality, the nostalgic tensions, all delicately sugared—drawn together by the benign homely voice in the blurb or on the screen.

This touching picture is an inexhaustible cultural document. Like all the advertisements which follow, it employs some of the most modern techniques of colour reproduction, and it is in composition, grouping and timing, expertly taken. The photographers have gone to school with experts; they have learned their historic function from Eugene Atget and Cartier-Bresson, and from the history of Western Art. Our anxious recoil from the manipulative intentions of the advertisements is slight in comparison with our unaffected admiration for how well it is done.* What is bled away from such photographs is of course the humanity of the people they portray. Not grossly, but delicately the fullness of colour, the high gloss of the finish throw a patina of glamour over the events and give them the magic

* I expand a point here made very shrewdly by Ian MacKillop, in a brief essay, 'The Eye of the Beholder', *Delta* (Cambridge) 32, Spring 1964.

and suggestiveness of the world which lies around the advertiser's corner. It is not simple to detect this. For in part, ordinary human creativeness being unquenchable, these photographs do figure an authentic response by some technician, earning his necessary living and voicing his necessary soul. There is consolation to be found in the evidence of so many accurate pictures that even when subtle techniques are hired by the forces of capital, those techniques insist on having their own say, laden with values which in a small way resist the context. But this is only true if we spend longer looking at the picture than is sure to be the case. His human sympathies notwithstanding, the photographer sees and frames what we all see. His field of perception is narrowly actual, and the actualities of dress, style, gesture, are what we have learned to read with immense rapidity and sureness in the busy traffic of urban living. We do not see with Dickens's eyes in the city:

They went quietly down into the roaring streets, inseparable and blessed; and as they passed along in sunshine and in shade, the noisy and the eager and the arrogant and the froward and the vain, fretted, and chafed, and made their usual uproar.*

There is no ready vocabulary in currency which describes this spiritual tumult. There is however a widespread, precise and enthusiastic habit of observation which ceaselessly records and judges surface life—fashion and manners. The absence of a moral vocabulary and the presence, so to speak, of a vocabulary of styles is a condition of our history; but the rhetoric of advertising has a decided and causal responsibility. I think these remarks hold for all the remaining illustrations.

The car advertisement (Plate 5) is less intrusive partly because its market is now so surely structured. Barclay's Bank were trying to capture a segment of the public ('young and looking to the future') who are not necessarily turning their way. British Leyland know much more confidently whom they are speaking to and can count also on the motor car's being a master symbol in our culture in its own right. There is no need, in the hateful jargon, to presell the customer. He will be interested enough anyway to enter the special vocabulary. But this is not an example of stage one on our scale, a simple announcement to an interested minority. For the car owner

* *Little Dorrit*, 1837, chap. 34.

Plate 8. Concorde

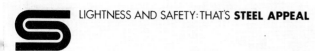

LIGHTNESS AND SAFETY: THAT'S **STEEL APPEAL**

Concorde lands on slim steel legs at over 170 m.p.h.
No other material is light enough!

Concorde touches down at 170 m.p.h. And it weighs 100 tons. As you'd imagine, its undercarriage legs have to be forged from an incredibly light, tough material.

They are. Those undercarriage legs are steel. Anything else would make them too heavy, too bulky. In steel, they're slim, light and fantastically strong.

That's the beauty of steel. It's got more strength, elasticity and precision than practically anything else you can think of. In fact, it's got what we call steel appeal.

British Steel Corporation

Plate 9. Mary Quant

Love is the great destroyer of the beautiful face.

Think of the hours you spend in front of the mirror.
Then think in just how few seconds your careful, painstaking work could go haywire.

This has worried Mary Quant.

Why should a girl look her most frightful when she should be looking her most beautiful?

And this is why she has come to your aid.

With incredible new cosmetics that love can't shift. Eye Tint colours. Six of them. They could stay put for 24 hours, if you like.

Lash Colours. Black and Brown Black. They don't smudge. They don't mark. They just do their work quietly, and make you lovely.

And Blush Sticks and Colour Sticks.

They look like foundation sticks, but they're not. They're new and different: make-up that colours your skin. But doesn't mask it.

Passion won't harm the remarkable effect.

But a good wash will remove it completely.

There's even a new Mary Quant perfume to match. It's called Potion, and unlike ordinary perfumes it's made with oil. Needless to say, oil does marvellous things to the skin, and the heady aroma lasts much longer than old-fashioned perfumes.

Finally, for lovers, Mary Quant Breath Fresheners. If you've gone to all the trouble to make yourself look good enough to eat, at least make sure you taste delicious.

All Mary Quant's new cosmetics are in the shops now. They're called 'Make-up to Make Love in'.

And she loved making them for you.

Mary Quant.
Make-up to Make Love in.
Make because you should look beautiful in love.

is customer to the most volatile and centrally placed industry in the economy. It fits best of all the classical model of oligopoly industries in modern capitalism in its need for the precise calculation of markets, rapid turnover and large surplus for reinvestment in retooled plant. To fit its drive onwards people need to change their cars regularly, and therefore within the closely stratified and class-based mass market, the car firms (on a mass scale there are only two national ones) constantly introduce minor modifications which imply the obsolescence of the alternatives. In this case, front wheel drive, a remounted engine, new garters, an extra 200 c.c., and 12 inches shorter than the unnamed 'American owned competition' (Buy British: Buy for Victory). The technical details are then placed beneath a photograph whose setting, high-speed blur and excitingly bad weather suggest the thrills of long-distance rallies, remote countrysides, and fast driving. It has long been noted how car promotion is heavily sexualized. The unforgettable consumer-Everyman of David Turner's play *Semi-Detached* ran briskly through the sexual and/or respectable overtones of car names—'the French Dauphine, the shy Gazelle, the Princess or the Minx—little Minnie, the Hawk, the Jaguar, and the Rapier' or 'the decent, respectable middle-aged man's Rover . . . Here Rover, good dog!' as well as his own Vanguard for the 'family on the march'.*

In spite of the new Hillman Avenger, promoted with a fraction of the £400,000 by supergirls in black scuba kit, the emphasis in car buying tends to be more technical, or rather, to use technical detail to suggest the old flagrant and irresponsible turns on the twist-point of power and lust. This is an interesting example taken from a report as opposed to an advertisement. It illustrates the closeness of the two in many publications. What purports to be a shopper's guide is, particularly for cars, often invisible promotion.

It is a full-blooded car that tosses new-fangled virtue like silence away on the winds of performance. It accelerates to 70 m.p.h. in 11 sec., it takes a he-man 47 lb. tread to work the clutch; and from 70 m.p.h. the windroar grows like a jumbo jet gathering power for take-off.†

The Concorde/B.S.C. advertisement (Plate 8) is one of an increasing number in the national dailies which occupy that ill-defined but

* David Turner, *Semi-Detached*, Methuen, 1962, p. 10.
† *Drive*, July 1970.

centrifugal zone of the economy which advertisers and their sponsors camouflage with prestige advertisements in the national interest. Once more, this is a still form of TV commercial which might as well have been a newscast. Again the blur suggests the colossal power and speed of the machine especially since the B.S.C. has paid for a large amount of empty (i.e. vast and immeasurable) sky at the top. The result is, in Raymond Williams' biting words, 'a system of mimed celebration of other people's decisions'.* Officially the British Aircraft and the British Steel Corporations are nationally owned and answerable to the nation. In fact, they are run from the small and unknown centres of power, and in the face of colossal losses on the aircraft, probable restrictions on its overland use and the problem of its noisiness, one corporation jacks up the next in the hope of dignifying the failure with some air of achievement.

The last example of this stage on our scale suggests its limitations, since it breaks with the accepted convention that the general atmosphere of the advertisement will enhance the product or service. In some ways this one suggests that the resources of advertisers will eventually run dry, because it turns upon itself and only works because of the convention established elsewhere. The Mary Quant two-pager (Plate 9) is an exceptionally choice instance and an illuminating example of fitting the ad to the audience, this time in *Honey*. The prevailing tone of *Honey* being what it is, frank, girl to girl, emancipated, uninhibited, swinging—a casebook of pop language—this advertisement can employ the same robust candour. 'Make-up to Make Love in'. Because, of course, that is how every hot-blooded girl spends her time now that the great name of freedom has been corralled and broken in on the side of sexuality ('after all, you wouldn't like to seem frigid, would you dear?'). Not that the girl is any more than prettily tousled and rather fetchingly guileless and deodorized about the mouth, but nor is she out of sight of the readers of *Honey*. Identification is easy, and so it is on the opposite page where another great name, Love, is monstrously equated in headlines with physical passion, and the manufacturers achieve the grisly triumph of binding a cosmetic with the two master-symbols of the ABC teenage markets. The text is more revolting the more you read it, in its brisk no-nonsense mixture of outspokenness and maternal firmness:

* Raymond Williams, 'Crisis in Communications', *Listener*, 31 July 1969, p. 138.

Finally, for lovers [or, as it were, 'there now, that's the lot, I think'] Mary Quant Breath Fresheners. If you've gone to all the trouble to make yourself look good enough to eat, at least make sure you taste delicious.

This catches exactly the worst register of a magazine which at other times can provide in a reach-me-down way useful commonsense for sixteen-year-olds who exchange little with their parents.

Stage 4. Subconscious or magic symbol advertising

This final stage marks the point at which the dissociation of rationality and feeling are complete and marks, too, the modulation of advertisements into a complete iconography. The whole manner of many photographs make it clear that they intend us to perceive them with a quite unassailable mixture of reverence, desire, aspiration, and passiveness. If we take the following text as representing a familiar mode, it is easy to invent the rather cluttered, self-indulgent and exotic picture that goes with it.

FANTASY. THE FIRST WARM FRAGRANCE FOR THE COOL
GENERATION.

Morny blended Fantasy for you—today's girl. And it smells deliciously like you. Warm, but coolly confident. Gentle, but sexy. You never smelled so pretty. Or felt so clean. Because Fantasy is not only Spray Mist, and Eau de Toilette. Fantasy is Soap, Talc and Bath Foam too. It doesn't cost the earth: department stores, Boots and other good chemists sell the Spray Mist for only 14/9d, and Fantasy soap for only 2/10d.

One knows the dreamy line by heart. Harrods and Spanish-Kensington antiques, masses of tumbling hair and spotless linen. By contrast, the manner of Plate 10 is altogether more brilliant and assured. The picture is suffused in a rosy brown, the girl is sensationally pretty in a very pensive way which combines with the muted lighting to give an extraordinary and powerful sense of innocence and sexual longing. The result is a blasphemous alliance of holiness with ogling. The stylish, caressing attention to light and posture fill the picture with this incense. The garishness and vulgarity of the bolstered belles in the forties have vanished and the much more penetrating scent of sweet and discreet sexuality lies on the air. As the catch puts it, however, 'it pays more to be a real whore'.

The same techniques irradiate the next two pictures with even greater irrelevance. At least the girl was wearing the bra. The picture of the steelworker (Plate 11) seems to me an outrageous insult. It is beautifully taken: the suggestion of inconceivable and satanic power in the rich coincidence of white-orange heat and blackness, the fine face picking up on the far, unexpected side the light, and the powerful forearm glowing golden on the same side, the realistic detail of the sweaty vest, the grimy cheek, the rivulets on the man's strong face— strongly marked and clefted, full of a lived, vivid experience. The photographer has learned from Rembrandt these dramatic concentrations of colour and light and he has thrown over the picture that high gloss which romanticizes the subject and puts at a distance the smell, the dirt, the destroying conditions of work. And this, these techniques, this man's life are called in the service of selling industrial lighting in a colour supplement!*

The advertisement for *The Times* (Plate 12) shows almost as complete a gap between atmosphere and content. Here again we have expert techniques in the service of irrelevance—a gay, alive picture of today's Beautiful People in a golf club acting as a straight but implicit statement that *The Times* is for and about such people, *is* folks, so long as they are AB1 social class folks in the 25–35 consumer age bracket. And what more could anyone want, this side of Paradise? The picture is elegantly composed—a sort of Caravaggio of our times, times which speak eloquently through the charming faces, the good clothes, the watch, the clubs and silver cups, all engaging and immediate like any group photograph will be, or indeed like any group will be seen from outside, as the copy reminds us.

A related but in this case less potent and more nearly fatuous kind of borrowing appears in the Rank Xerox series which reproduced in two-page spreads very slightly esoteric but faultlessly fashionable paintings as an analogue for their own xerographic reproduction techniques. The link between subject and content was very tenuous but the real meaning of the advertisement lay in the juxtaposition of (for example) the expensive but not-quite-well-known painter De Staël and his picture 'The Footballers' with the earnest smiling

---

* See page 131 for a defence of this advertisement supplied by Thorn Lighting's advertising agent.

service of Rank Xerox. The power and the roughness of the original painting was reduced to comfortable size and texture and the advertiser, once more, successfully employed a bold, idiosyncratic art-work in the service of consumption. Here, in the most visible way, art has become the commodity which the auction market has made it. The appeal by the firm to the art they hire for the advertisement helps the conversion of art-values into cash-values, and the process is an integral part of the picture of art and knowledge circulated by advertising. In I.C.I.'s 'image-building' Pathfinder series of TV commercials they make a similar appeal to another master-symbol— social concern for world poverty which is a function of the guilt of the rich West over the terrible poverty of Asia and Africa. The series, memorably filmed, showed I.C.I.'s technological contributions to the irrigation and fertilizing of desert Asia. We are not, of course, told of the terms on which the contributions are made, terms the general nature of which are perhaps hinted at in this report from the *New York Times* in April 1966:

There are signs of change. The Government has granted easy terms to private foreign investors in the fertilizer industry, is thinking about decontrolling several more industries and is ready to liberalize import policy if it gets sufficient foreign aid ... Much of what is happening now is a result of steady pressure from the United States and the International Bank for Reconstruction and Development, which for the last year have been urging a substantial freeing of the Indian economy and a greater scope for private enterprise. The United States pressure, in particular has been highly effective here because the United States provides by far the largest part of the foreign exchange needed to finance India's development and keep the wheels of industry turning. Call them 'strings', call them 'conditions' or whatever one likes, India has little choice but to agree to many of the terms that the United States, through the World Bank, is putting on its aid. For India simply has nowhere else to turn.

Indeed the whole question of aid from the giant international corporations is one which there is not the opportunity to develop here. It is nonetheless in this context that we might recall Hugh Scanlon's pointing out* that recent forecasts claim that by 1990 only two hundred multinational firms will account for over 75 per cent of the total corporate assets of the capitalist world. These firms invest these

* 'International Combines versus the Unions', *Bulletin of the Institute for Workers' Control*, Nottingham, 1, 4, 1969.

assets, deploy, reclaim and reinvest them throughout the world in such ways that

United States Corporations and their multinational subsidiaries currently control between 70–90 per cent of the raw material resources of Latin America, and more than 60 per cent of its industrial plant. Its public utilities, its banking, commerce and foreign trade relationships are in the hands of U.S. Corporations or their subsidiaries.*

A similar analysis holds true for British firms in Africa, and this at a time when the gap between famine and wealth is getting steadily wider.† It is in this frame that we should judge the prestige advertising programmes.

But of course the whole point of such a commercial as the I.C.I. 'Pathfinder' is that the flow of information is in one way only; the controllers select the information and can make their appeals to unselfishness and altruism without having to mention the shareholders' dividend. The giant corporation which as we have seen in Chapter Three will on other occasions insist on its exclusive rights to planning its profits is able to lay straight-faced claim to be seen as a benevolent welfare concern. It thus keeps up the good work of selling short the national conscience. 'With I.C.I. around, what need of overseas aid?' The line of such commercials was produced into infinity by the 1968 presidential campaign in the U.S.A. where the use of highly sophisticated and utterly lethal spot advertising by Messrs Nixon and Humphrey did such public damage to the idea of democracy as public debate and shared argument. Nixon spent twenty million dollars‡ in making clear how ruthlessly the belief in mass manipulation unites big business and power politics.

Closing the circle of ideas

The main axis along which I have laid the analysis has been technical. The four stages represent a very rough guide to the relation between form and content, information and illustration, reason and feeling,

* F. Clairmonte, *Economic Liberalism and Under-development*, Bombay, Asia Publishing House, 1960, p. 54.
† See G. Adler-Karlsson, *Western Economic Warfare 1947–67*, Stockholm, 1968.
‡ Cf. Joe McGuinness, *The Selling of the President*, André Deutsch, 1970.

and so on. This classification gives us a way into an advertisement and its intentions. We then go on to measure the gap between statement and meaning. There are other dimensions to consider. There is the division by sex: is the advertisement intended for men or women? There are the divisions by class, the difference between Mary Quant in *Honey* and *19*, and *Vogue* or *Queen*. There are the divisions by age: is the advertisement intended for over forties or under forties? Finally and importantly there are the divisions by symbolic appeal. That is, do the advertisements appeal to established values in our culture, or do they speak to thwarted longings?

The advertisers have already made many of these decisions and we need to remake them in order to understand their intentions. We need the further classifications in order to come at the full social meanings of the advertisements, and use them to tell us all they will about our society.

Advertisements group themselves in the categories of modern society. Their whole technique serves to settle the divisions which already exist between social classes, between the sexes and between the generations. The fantasies and prizes which the advertisements hold out are precisely adjusted to the further limits to which their audience can aspire, but they never suggest (how could they?) that any other way of living or any other kind of social relations would be imaginable. Even at their most fantastic, the fantasies grow straight out of the existing constellations of wealth, power and privilege. Thus the circle of ideas and images put in incessant motion by advertising short-circuits any contradiction. There is no point of insertion at which we can say 'no!'. The surface of this circle is smooth and impassive; every idea or image intersects with another and curves round to meet itself. All the explanations of behaviour which lie within the language confirm themselves, they make themselves true by definition. Consider a list of typical ideas:

picturesquerie (countryside *and* rugged workman)
youth culture and young love
domesticity, babies, children, ordinariness
group togetherness
love and sexuality
acquisition and possession
national interest and prestige (i.e. more money according to the present rates
of distribution)
conspicuous consumption

Various assortments of these key ideas penetrate all advertisements and connect them with all other advertisements no matter how varied the content may appear to be. This is what we mean by 'the closed circle of ideas' or 'the magic system'. Thus, motor cars combine several of the key ideas—sometimes love and sexuality (he-man sports cars), sometimes family togetherness, always possession and acquisition. High art may be used to combine national prestige and lavish spending, or it may combine cosmetics and well-bred sherry; in either case its traditional value works to tie prestige, purchase, and ostentation inextricably together. Sexual incitement is rarely absent from advertising, but again it always defines itself in relation to objects —most obviously, clothes and cosmetics. Consequently every advertisement which appeals to sexual feelings ends up by reducing women to the status of objects—objects to be acquired and possessed by men. What is more, the advertisements imply that this is how women want to see themselves: as desirable and beautiful possessions. Since this is clearly a cruel insult if women saw what was being said, the advertisements suffuse the sexual possessiveness with haunting plangencies, remoteness and mystery. The beautiful women become *piétas* of sexuality and objects of worship. It is a queer transformation of that late Victorianism in which real women were widely seen in the conventional ideology as 'perfect wives and mothers', figures on a pedestal. In the advertisements they become perfect versions of the sex kitten or the Snow Queen or the little-girl-lost or whatever notion of desirability has currency at a given time. And so, sexual feeling and action become an adjunct of the economy. The rapid and resourceful exploitation of sexual change makes a classic case study in any appraisal of the techniques of advertising. For advertising probably does *not* create social action from nothing. But to be successful it must recognize the developing actions which signal change and capture and shape these in its own interests. The process then compounds itself, as we have seen, and society takes on a headlong impetus towards mass consumption, forever insatiable. I outlined this in the first chapter. Gradually purchase, consumption, and always rising expectations root themselves in a society's moral sensibility. Now the change in sexual behaviour during the last thirty or forty years started out from many places—from the first world war, from the decline in religious beliefs, from industrialization and the rise of secularism, from increased physical mobility, from heaven knows elsewhere. Because sexual feeling is so profound a part of any person and because sexual action in the nineteenth century expressed itself so completely in class terms (as witness the colossal numbers of prostitutes in London*) the changes signalled in sexual behaviour might have been a source of large-scale social change. Yet without conscious conspiracy all the machinery of the mass manipulators has worked to cut off this area of experience from society until the changes of feeling which might (for good and bad) have altered human relations in our society, rearranged themselves within the terms of the mass market. Now we are asked to see sexuality in the terms of acquisitiveness.

No doubt this account simplifies very complex movements, yet it explains some parts of social change and gives rise to a proposition: advertising tries to organize broad social tendencies in precise and profitable directions. As we have already said, it can only do this insofar as its ways of thinking, speaking and valuing affect the mass communication system in its totality, and the way in which this, in turn, affects people's lives.

* See also Steven Marcus, *The Other Victorians*, Weidenfeld, 1968.

FIVE

The Effects of Advertising

The argument about 'effects' is by now notoriously difficult and much contested. When, for example, a market researcher talks about the 'effects' of a particular advertising campaign he means, in the cant, 'post-exposure consumption patterns'; in other words describing how people have bought the product in question once they have heard about it. He can only guess intelligently (or otherwise) at the reasons for the behaviour, just as the television researcher can only guess at many of the motives which cause people to behave in certain ways *after* (and not necessarily *because*) they have been watching certain programmes. But this latter kind of research is bound to be more speculative, though none the worse for that, because it is trying to perceive changes in attitudes and behaviour which move slowly and register themselves in impalpable ways. The market researcher is happy so long as after the campaign the people buy his stuff. We need instead to penetrate further in an attempt to see the long-term shifts in values and moral language which we see as the results not of advertising alone (which would be much too nerveless of us) but of the whole tendency of a society much of whose essential energy springs from a need to buy, consume, throw away, and buy again— a need which is not innate though it is certainly widely shared but just as certainly serves most devoutly the interests of a few men in a very few countries of the world. To achieve such imaginative penetration we need to envision 'effects' across a very long and broad field. We need to see the effects through a long period of time and also across a whole field of perception—moral, verbal, imaginative, as well as simply visual or aural. This means, as we have tried to show, taking in historical and sociological areas much more fully than a simple study of stimulus ('look at this picture; don't you feel thirsty?') and response ('yes; buy me a coke') can ever do. But such an ambitious enterprise means that our generalizations must be sometimes vague (as opposed to much too local), or alternatively speculative, the diagnosis of imaginative understanding rather than the much clumsier kind available to the methods of empiric inquiry.

There are three areas in which we may study effects. The first is the mass communication system itself. How far have the assumptions and intentions of advertising affected the language and values of the mass media?

The effects on the media

In one way the entire book up to this point has tried to answer this enormous question. The effects on the media are obvious. Advertising is the main source of revenue for *all* printed periodicals and newspapers and for half the televised information, culture and entertainment in the country. A commercial presence appears about every fifteen minutes on television and on almost every page of everyone's dailies and weeklies. This effect of advertising is present everywhere, and we have tried to account for it in terms of its origins, economics, politics, as well as its significance in the culture of individual men and women. But in a more limited and also less visible way advertising—or, better, commercialism, alters and diverts the information and opinions which reach us with apparent innocuity along the swift channels of television or print. One alteration is the reports of the decisions and appointments of senior businessmen and financiers as though they were TV celebrities. It is a confusion which Wright Mills classically analyses in *The Power Elite*:

Yet prestige is the shadow of money and power. Where these are, there it is. Like the national market for soap or automobiles and the enlarged arena of federal power, the national cash-in area for prestige has grown, slowly being consolidated into a truly national system. Since the men of the higher political, economic, and military circles are an élite of money and power, they accumulate a prestige that is considerably above the ordinary; all of them have publicity value and some of them are downright eminent; increasingly, by virtue of their position and by means of conscious public relations, they strive to make their names notable, their actions acceptable, their policies popular. And in all this they tend to become national celebrities.

Members of the power élite are celebrated because of the positions they occupy and the decisions they command. They are celebrities because they have prestige, and they have prestige because they are thought to have power or wealth. It is true that they, too, must enter the world of publicity, become material for the mass media, but they are sought as material almost irrespective of what they do on and to these media.*

We have already remarked something of the kind in the 1968 U.S. presidential campaign. Insofar as the centres of power have shifted in Britain into the hands of the corporations and the discount houses, then this following piece of reporting seems thoroughly sinister.

A soft-spoken, grey-haired fifty-two-year old, Hunt is a firm disciple of North American business methods . . . Apart from the Rolls Royce Phantom V, Buick and Triumph 2000 he keeps in his stable, Hunt knows little about cars. But when it comes to questions of productivity and business methods, he is in his element.†

This is about the Managing Director of Rootes. The profile features in various business reports is of a piece with this. As, for instance, here:

Michael Pickard has made good use of his 16 years in industry—apart from the three months he took off work to have 'a number of very good games of golf', after a boardroom tiff. He has, as a former colleague puts it, a 'knack of being at the right place at the right time with the right people.'

The right place now is the managing director's chair in the new £100 million Trust Houses Forte combine, which has made Pickard, who is 37, one of the most powerful young men in British industry. Yet in some ways Pickard, who has risen at a meteoric pace from a City chartered account-ants office to head the country's biggest hotel and entertainments group, has still to prove himself.

Admiringly, we follow with the journalist the great man's progress.

Again, he had the opportunity to build from scratch, and again he had moved on through his 'old friends' network. As Ronald Edwards says: 'Michael Pickard's good fortune is that he has worked with friends all along.' Pickard reciprocated the gesture by opening the way for his old school friend, Richard Botwood, to take his job at Melbray.

There is much to say about how such connections are maintained through the corridors of British and American financial power, but

* C. Wright Mills, *The Power Elite*, Oxford, 1956, p. 83.
† *Financial Times*, 22 March 1967.

more to our point is the way the man is reported to us, the uncritical admiration of power, promotion, wealth, and keeping one's social subordinates in their place:

So, for the first time, Pickard stepped from the shadow behind a managing director's throne to sit on it himself. 'It was,' says an associate, 'a job for a big man.' Pickard, a hefty 6 ft. 5 in. who keeps in trim playing squash or village cricket near his palatial home (formerly owned by an Eastern potentate) near Reigate in Surrey, certainly fits this bill.

'One of his great qualities,' says Richard Botwood, 'is that he turns out with the village side, who are mostly a lot of local farmers, just as if he was an accountant in a Trust House subsidiary—not the managing director of the whole show. He's never grown out of the village cricket.' His other interests include rugby and sitting on the governing body at Roedean.*

A prime effect of the age of mass communications, as these little examples suggest, is to mix up politicians, entertainers, news makers and businessmen, and with varying emphases to give them pride of place as the public heroes of society. Consequently, much reporting, like many of the prestige advertisements, becomes indeed mimed celebration of the rulers' decisions. Reporting the financial world in these ways is a new development: it is only recently that the most powerful businessmen have won their places on *Any Questions?*, *24 Hours*, *Late Night Line-Up*, or the other broadcast forums of instant platitude; the terrific expansion of the business sections is a part of the same process and, humanly enough, the individuals in question enjoy their own newsiness. But the more general process of which they are symptoms works to keep the circles of thought closed. It becomes harder and harder to disentangle the celebrations of commercialism from the descriptions. Advertising is the systematic voice of commercialism. Getting its rhetoric straight gives us a base against which to test the other forms of public speaking for contamination. For the connections are surprisingly close between the big-time entertainers who have completely captured a docile audience, and the controllers of wealth and power. The overwhelming cant of the pop scene obscures the way in which its ideology of success and public consumption—the 'higher immorality'—contradicts nothing of the quieter accents in the business sections. The fabulous wealth of the pop stars, their dashing clothes and high-flying life-styles, their bumbling and unexceptionable public-utterances-become-scripture,

* *Sunday Times Business Section*, 10 May 1970.

fit very easily into the system. The impulse to change or to dissent which may be latent in teenage action now seems pretty safely accommodated, for the time being at least.

The accommodation can be seen in many places. When the format of the *Radio Times* changed in 1969, the insertion of glossy full page colour photographs concentrated on the pop world (and the cult hagiology, from Jean Harlow to Marilyn Monroe) in a style which came straight from the TV and colour-supplement commercials. Confusion between history and fantasy is compounded in these pages by presenting characters from leading serials as real people. In the *TV Times* for 11 September 1970, Len Fairclough of *Coronation Street* gets a full-page colour picture and a brief life-history just as though he, too, were a member of the jet set. The same happens to the hero of *The Virginian* in the *Radio Times* for 20 August 1970, although this time the colour photograph carries with it the subtlest innuendo of nostalgia for the lost pin-up magazines of Hollywood's heyday in the forties. In this way the cult periods, the *piétas* and talismans of the past come in a period of manipulated consumer change nearer and nearer the present. The function of the past is not in any sense to provide perspectives on the present; it merely stimulates a nostalgia, the soft pallid sentimentality of which is the obverse of the hardboiled hedonism of the today people. *They* appear in profusion on either the feature and editorial or the advertisement pages of all the weeklies and many of the popular TV serials. Their book of hours is the colour-supplement, which where it does not dissolve the separation of content and advertisement until it has vanished permits a casual juxtaposition of the two which is on occasion simply revolting. During the slaughter of the West African war between Nigeria and secessionist Biafra a colour supplement set *side-by-side* a very large picture of a blazing truck with bullet holes in it and the arm of a still living though badly wounded Ibo woman thrust out from the door, together with another large picture of a dreamy, sexy pair of conspicuous consumers mooning along beside a twilit sea and a snappy new sportscar. The colours, the expert technique of the two pictures, were identical. The clear, doubtless unintended invitation was to an utter and degrading moral idiocy.

It was an extreme example of a general repetition which results from the unobstructed invasion of what we shall know as human beings by the intolerable requirements of other people that we shall know our humanity only through our purses. In an exceptionally developed example, a number of the *Daily Telegraph* colour supplement (252, 8 August 1969) collapses every one of the decent-spirited liberal's social anxieties into the warm mess of mass consumption. A few photographs which masquerade as feature but list products and retailers at the bottom show two models, both women, one a Negress, the other an Aryan blonde, showing off their breasts and their unzipped wet-look black boilersuits and boots in the blitzed deserts of downtown Cardiff. The whole egregious offering is, again, closed in its defences on every side by cast-iron cynicism. Consider the scenario. Very expensive, very sexy imitations of working-class working clothes being worn by very overpaid girls, one of them a member of a still brutally exploited race, in surroundings which are among some of the most rotten and squalid in Britain. And when the unlikely reader rises up in conscientious outrage his bluster is neatly turned by this unforgettable quotation from a producer of the goods and spokeswoman for this highly profitable culture:

I love vulgarity: good taste is death. Vulgarity is life. The erogenous zone of our present fashion period is the crutch. This is a very balanced generation and clothes are designed to lead the eye naturally to the crutch. The way girls model clothes, the way they sit, sprawl or stand, is all doing the same thing.

Mary Quant.

After this high peak of double and triple-talking, anything will seem flat. But it is still worth suggesting how deeply the ethic expressed and broadcast by advertising penetrates so many areas of imaginative life where we might not look out for it. One major change in British and American social life since 1945 has been the alleged arrival at independence of the teenagers and students. They see themselves and are seen as a social group in their own right. No doubt they are right. But their autonomy is hemmed right in by the terms in which they choose—or are coerced—to define it. In some ways *Honey* and *19* strike one as really innovating publications.

Honey, with its total devotion to the teenage world and its resounding echoes of pop, brought other things apart from fashion: a new 'realism', a disarming frankness, a new range of idols and models—David McCullum, the Rolling Stones, Andrew Oldham, Terry Stamp, The Who. And it brought some new attitudes ... Fluid and open, yes: but certainly not classless. *Honey* is for working girls of any class—but working girls with money to spend and a developed sense of sophistication in clothes, tastes and fashion.★

★ Stuart Hall, 'Class and the Mass Media' in *Class*, R. Mabey, ed., Blond, 1967, p. 108.

Our morale booster: it gives a pretty uplift.

We call it the Wonderbra.
In a lovely new colour – coco. Or black
or white.
Style No. 0793* costs about 50/- and
comes in sizes A32 to 36, B32 to 38 /C34
to 38 in black or white only).
Nobody understands a girl like we do. *Gossard*

Some places it takes guts to work in.

Blood, toil, tears and sweat. All too often, they're necessary for the human good.

Which doesn't mean they're good for the human body. Or for the lighting which enables the body to see where it's working.

Heat. Steam. Dirt. And worse. They're enough to make ordinary factory lighting not only inoperative, but downright dangerous.

Hence the Atlas Invincible range of fluorescent lighting.

Each Invincible fitting is extraordinarily tough. And each has been designed to overcome a particular problem or combination of problems.

For example, if you run a brewery or a plating shop, your biggest worry will be humidity.

Hygiene will be your headache in the processed food business.

We have an Invincible fitting to meet all common hazards.

We've gone about designing them with the kind of thoroughness you expect from Thorn.

The Thorn Technical Sales Force can advise you on the right Invincible fitting for your needs.

This coupon will bring you their instant attention.

As you'd expect from Thorn, their services are entirely free.

And, as Thorn expects from them, entirely expert.

To Thorn
Lighting Ltd.,
Thorn House,
Upper Saint
Martin's Lane,
London, W.C.2.
I would like to
know more about
the Atlas
Invincible range,
and how it can help
in overcoming our lighting problems.
Please get in touch with me immediately.

Twin tube
flameproof fitting.

Name
Position
Company
Address

Atlas Invincible from
Thorn Lighting

A member of the Thorn Group.   LL/IN1   A21

Plate 12. The Times

Remember how strange it felt the first time you walked in?

You may have taken a while actually getting around to joining your club.

Much as the people who belonged enjoyed it, maybe you thought it wasn't right for you. Then you became a member. Your first evening there was a bit strange because it was unfamiliar and you didn't know your way around.

But that feeling soon wore off. In no time at all you were perfectly at home in surroundings that were stimulating, satisfying and just plain enjoyable. Now you're glad you joined.

Couldn't the same be true of The Times?

You'll get on with The Times.
TODAY'S GREAT NEWSPAPER.

Hall comments disappointedly at the end of the essay in which he makes these remarks that when the media confront change 'they find it all too easy to shuffle from one set of simplifications to another'. We must not fall into equal simplifications of diagnosis, but if *Honey* does speak in some ways for a new social force, its voice has to be raised above a tremendous clamour of hucksters' voices in the same pages (72 of the 123 pages in the September 1970 issue; of the remaining 51, 20 feature articles on cosmetics and fashion). When it tries to find its own style amidst this babel in which 'style' and 'image' are probably the most used words, one lead story (September 1969) told in a quite accurate and extended way, exhibits again that painful confusion of moral values and lavish possessions which is the mark of commercialism. In the story a pair of estranged lovers meet again by chance just when the girl has heard that her mother is dying very quickly of cancer and that she is herself pregnant by another man whom she does not want to marry. The novel candour and real tensions of this situation are at once strained by the limits of self-aware emancipation and frankness. The cool, strained-hedonist style of the story is completed by a wholly unself-aware series of inventories of wealth and attractiveness—the knowing appraisal of the girls' tan, figure, swimsuit, way of walking; the details of hi-fi and good sherry in the Florida penthouse, the cigarette play. The writer carries off his tale as a very adroit harmony of decent guy with shrewd consumer.

In the sister publication *19* (97 pages out of 140 straight advertising in the September 1970 number) this film review catches the magazine at another moment at which a traditional morality, a straightforward, honest girlishness, and a hopeless susceptibility to style and gesture and fashion all intersect.

The gangster heroes of *Borsalino* (Jean-Paul Belmondo and Alain Delon) are death-defyingly attractive, elegant as well-designed machine guns, slickly dressed, amusing, violent, dashingly charming and immoral. So is the film. Set in Marseilles in the Thirties, it chronicles the rise of two engaging, small-time, bar-room criminals to the dual control of the Marseilles underworld, via a reckless and trigger-delirious career. Delon and Belmondo must be two of the world's most desirable men—the one undeniably beautiful, arrogant, sulky-mouthed and clear-eyed; the other beaten-up and humorous, leggy and tousle-headed.

This zippy, fluent prose possesses a superficial vitality which seems not to have roots in any recognizable life. The terms spring straight from the clichés of the fashion-pages—'amusing', 'slickly dressed', 'sulky mouth'—they then hit up against some notion of a link between style and image and the solid realities of the life the film parodies.

Occasionally, the realization of the unstinted violence and murder sours the dancing stylish charm that characterizes the film,

The clear suggestion is that this reality ought not to sour the 'dancing stylish charm' and that the art of the film like the art of the ad is to entrance with light fantasies. But there is fantasy and fantasy. There are films like *8½* and *Les Parapluies de Cherbourg*; there is on the other hand the fantasy which masks and glamorizes brutality by its attention to style and gesture, and this fantasy corroborates the technology of endless production and destruction.

The confusion of the new hedonism (swinging, classless) with genuine forms of liberation repeats itself time and again through the mass media, and whether the confusion is planned or accidental it is as certainly symptomatic as for a few people it is profitable. Pop idolatry very soon sounds like old, pre-war gossip columnist snobbery:

It was raining heavily when I reached the Wyngarde flat, on the ground floor of a Georgian house off London's Kensington High Street. Debbie—a breathtaking, if more than slightly dizzy, model in her early twenties—opened the front door, hurriedly kissed my cheek and rushed back to the lounge where Peter was lying across the buttoned leather couch looking tanned and terrific. The tan came from two months in Australia where his series has topped everything else in the ratings. It wasn't too difficult for him to look terrific as our favourite blonde laid herself beside him, closed her eyes, and wrapped her arms around him as if the moment had to be savoured. (*19*).

There isn't space here to develop an extended comparison between this sort of advertisement life and the values and life-styles carried by the older women's magazines. I can only suggest that such comparative studies can release a great deal about social values and the directions of change, and further that they should not be confined to periodicals. Even a casual reader of the *Guardian* over the past two or three years must have noticed the marked reduction in print and the increase in the size of photographs. The arts page may now feature a 15" × 12" close-up photograph of a writer whose books would not be given a third as much space in review. The change, I conjecture, is far more due to a mythology of mass communication than to any knowledge of 'what the readers want' (*Le Monde* for example has no pictures in many issues, each issue about 32 pages in length; *New York Herald Tribune* has only 14 in 14 pages, the biggest $4\frac{1}{2}'' \times 3\frac{1}{2}''$). This mythology has taken it for granted that the capture of the larger audience necessary to survival means that you must have more and bigger pictures in the idiom not of 'deer through October mist in Richmond Park' but of the TV close-up taken from below the jaw. It is easy to track down this sort of development in the format and news coverage of several local and national dailies. But the main territory for such comparative discrimination, difficult though it is to capture, is TV. I have suggested earlier how the success of the BBC's *The Forsyte Saga* in 1968–70 was achieved. It is obviously important to see what values are carried by the most successful TV serials and how far the style and imagery of the advertising world fills them. That it clearly does influence them strongly is obvious when we watch London Weekend's *Doctor in the House*, ITV's *The Avengers*, BBC's *Troubleshooters* (the Mogul programme), *Pick of the Pops*, or any variety show.

Analysis of a culture is never a put-up-knock-down job. Along with crashing sentimentality and the openness of such scenes to 'domestic' advertising, a passage like this from *Woman* has its contact with a continuing morality.

They had changed, he decided, but Ruth was right: Laurie had changed less than the rest of them. Being married to him, having babies, being stuck in a small town, couldn't have been all that bad. He got up for a cigarette and, from the other side of the room, while lighting it, studied them critically.

There was no denying that Ruth was now a handsome, sophisticated, young woman and Tom Moore was the budding executive. And no doubt at all that Laurie was a young wife and mother type. But it was Laurie, not they, who gave off the glow.

The meal was a good one; trust Laurie for that. She never failed to make him proud of her at times like this, and he knew darned well it wasn't all that easy; she just had a way of making it seem so.

All through dinner they talked of the old days, of the people they had known at high school and where they were now.

22 August 1970

In an unusual way this story challenges and explicitly rejects the ethic of competitive success. It comes down like the Evelyn Home column, on the side of a homespun and sometimes rigid domesticity. The story tries to have things both ways: it is the mother with the safe and dowdy life who is given the 'glow'; the tribute the husband pays to her is unctuous. But it is hard to imagine the swinging hedonists of some advertisements in the same journal finding congenial company here or in the agony columns.

It is a very complex and tentative business assigning causes to the presence of commercialism in the media. Sometimes it is unmistakable: we can point at *Mogul* or the fashion features of *Honey* or *Vogue* and see commercialism clearly. But the essential analysis is to discern the shifts in language and gesture which indicate a shift in meaning. We need to see how the steady distortion of the symbols and established meanings like love or warmth or friendship or, indeed, success and possession, in all the advertisements and the media generally, *causes* the loss of essential touchstones in our culture. It is important not to be misunderstood here. Words do change their meanings, because values change. What we must know is what, if anything, we lose when the change occurs. And we must count the cost. At this point we must relate the possible effects upon the mass media to the discernible effects which the social scientists have noted in people's behaviour.

The effects on behaviour

This is a very uncertain section. Much of its detail derives from research which directs itself towards single instruments like television, the conclusions of which can be generally applied. The research has been about ideas ('conceptual') and it has tried to uncover individual actions and the regular lines they follow ('empiric'). There has been a main demolition of the idea that we know TV supplies what people want because they watch it. This is the journalist's error who concluded that people wanted a certain soap-powder because they bought it. This conclusion misses out a whole range of conditions like availability, familiarity, presentation, absent-mindedness, attitude to advertising or medium, education, social class, and on and on. In the same way, vast audiences for certain TV programmes doesn't mean that every member of them likes that programme best, or even at all. Similarly another myth which the research has dismantled has been the belief that television directly affects how people take decisions—for example in their voting behaviour.* TV provides them with more political information, but one cannot say that it *causes* a change of heart. Granted that advertising is much less acrimoniously reasonable than politics on British TV and much more insidious, it is still encouraging that this kind of resistance seems to obtain. The general lesson to be learned† is that there can be no question of adequately discussing the effects of the mass media if we concentrate on one-to-one effects, single studies of marketing campaigns and voting behaviour. We have to follow through such diffuse factors as the individual psychology and morality, what he sees of what is in front of him, and what he remembers; we have to observe what social groups he belongs to and what his groups believe in; we have to trace, as we have seen Lazarsfeld do, the lines of communication between these groups from friend to neighbour or colleague, and we have to spot the leaders of opinion. All this effort shows the impossibility of discovering the *social effects* of advertising in any hard and fast way, though we may be able to measure the *effectiveness*‡ of single messages. It is a matter of commonsense that television in particular puts in circulation altered pictures of the world and that its amazing resourcefulness (e.g. the slow-motion instant playback) its immediacy and interstellar range, its up-to-dateness, all make it an instrument of unrivalled potency. To weigh and value this presence and its relation to newspapers, magazines, radio, and then the relation of all these to advertising requires us—as I attempt to do in this study—to respond as closely as we can to the particular advertisements and then to bed them deeply in their cultural context, in the conventions which make them intelligible and the intentions the advertiser would have us perceive as well as those he would not. Within this framework it will be worth setting out such social effects of the mass media as seem to be valid and which bears on people's likely uses of advertising.

Study after study confirms what we know: that people's leisure time has radically revised since the arrival of television. It seems not to have lead to any widening of interests, especially amongst children. Heavy viewers are less selective, watch much more commercial

---

* This synopsis of research work comes from J. D. Halloran, *The Effects of Mass Communication*, Leicester University Press 1965. It also is worth studying Dr Halloran's *Attitude Formation and Change*, New York: Humanities Press, 1967, and H. Krugman, 'The Impact of TV Advertising', *Public Opinion Quarterly*, XXXIX, 3, 1965.

† Cf. J. Trenaman and D. McQuail, *Television and the Political Image*, Methuen, 1961.

‡ The terms are Dr Halloran's in *The Effects of Television*, Panther, 1970.

television and are, by the present criteria, the less intelligent and the less well-off.*

With these conclusions in mind, it is very threatening to learn that television may 'narcotize rather than energize'† and may produce a listless social conformism and passive acceptance of things-as-they-are. As I have insisted here, the two researchers also point out mildly, 'the commercially-sponsored mass media indirectly but effectively restrain... a genuinely critical outlook'. The general conclusions which transpire are these‡:

1. Mass communication is not usually a direct cause but works its effects slowly through existing conditions.
2. It tends to reinforce existing conditions, because people are much more sympathetic to what they want to hear or see and ignore much of the rest.
3. When mass communication does affect people directly, it is generally those who are most exposed and solitary (e.g. the old and the very young, or disturbed people).
4. When social change of some kind is on the way, mass communications can help it along.
5. Mass communications are very much the product of their own technology and their own controllers and systems of organization. There is nothing neutral about them.

It is not hard to relate these conclusions directly to the effects of advertising and to say at the risk of tedious repetition that the study of advertising must be long term, must try to take in the whole movement of a society and its culture as well as marking out a whole frame of perception. When it does, then the generalizations are likely to hold good: that people do come to see intense buying and consuming (rather than using and keeping) as a part of their morality; that they do see objects as symbols of their own prestige and promotion; that they do convert their notion of the old luxury into the new necessity; lastly and grimly, that they accept the control of mass communications

---

* All summarized in Halloran (1965). The important texts are: Lyle, Schramm, Parker, *Television in the Lives of our Children*, Oxford, 1961, and Hilde Himmelweit et al., *Television and the Child*, Oxford, 1958, together with the ITV and BBC annual handbooks.

† P. F. Lazersfeld and Merton 'Mass Communications, Popular Taste and Organized Social Action' in W. Schramm ed. *Mass Communications*, Illinois, 1960.

‡ Paraphrased from J. T. Klapper, *The Effects of Mass Communications*, Glencoe Free Press, 1961.

by a few men whose central concern is to organize society to make
money for them.

NB. *The effectiveness of campaigns*

It is in this frame that we must place a tiny selection of the unbelievably
vast amount of specifically commercial research. What is remarkable
about a bibliography which has been estimated at 14,000 items
emanating (in Britain and the U.S.A.) from over fifty periodicals is how
little work there is on the direct effects of particular campaigns.
Nearly all the immense labour and expense goes on the 'presell': on
identifying the very precise targets at whom the product is aimed
and determining the possible size of demand. Within these limits, the
inquiries rarely do more than rely upon doorstep answers to interview
schedules. All the familiar objections to such methods rise up at once.
Do people tell the truth? (yes, apparently). Do they remember clearly?
Does conscious recollection matter anyway? Certainly their interest
in the TV commercials varies according to their interest in the programme as you would expect* but casual practices like going out to
make the tea during the breaks are widespread. Even at peak hours
many people will not be watching a set while it is on (25 per cent of
housewives asked†); many others will be doing other things like
ironing in the same room (40 per cent). People may remember
advertisements but they appear not to alter their actions as a result.
For instance, a group of children who all remembered road safety
television spots did not change their road habits as a result.* The
crude dilemma, as one theoretician points out,† is to divide people
into two groups:

(i) those who are aware of the advertising campaign,
(ii) those who are not

and then discover the proportion of product buyers in group (i). This
will show you the effectiveness of the campaign. But this is pretty
spongy. What does 'aware of' mean? What about the 'point-of-sale'
—shop, supermarket, salesman and so on? How do people move

---

* See *Research in Advertising*, Market Research Society, 1963, pp. 7, 17–27, 49.
† See also Dan Ingman, *Television Advertising*, London Business Publications, 1965.

from (ii) to (i)? It is at this point that our happy ignorance about the human mind undermines so much inquiry, and makes the argument about effects much more important at a general, cultural level than in these tiny manoeuvres. On the basis of the existing research, a contributor to an advertising* symposium suggested this familiar list of possibilities:

1. A consumer believes advertisements which remind him of what he knows.
2. A single advertisement will not change his behaviour.
3. Any change is tentative and may be revoked.
4. Every consumer is quite capable of weighing up advertising claims rationally, especially when changing his behaviour.

If we take these guarded sentences and compare them with the wild claims made by the official spokesmen then we may recover our nerve a little. In another useful book† which presents a series of case-studies Messrs Harris and Seldon set the growth of sales alongside the increase of advertising. The famous Milk Marketing Board campaign which culminated with 'Drinka Pinta Milka Day' succeeded a rise in advertising expenditure from £390,000 in 1956–57 to £1,315,000 in 1960–61. A decline in milk consumption stopped and then turned upwards from the (relatively!) low point of 1,337 million gallons per year to a record 1,409 million. Considering the quantities, not an enormous rise, but one which seemed directly related to the campaign. Harris and Seldon make similar claims in their case-study of the Hoover washing machine campaigns. After large-scale marketing, ownership of these rose from 2 per cent of the total population in 1948 to 23 per cent in 1957 to 45 per cent in 1961 to 55 per cent in 1968. Hoover now commands over 70 per cent of the market, a command which has involved a consistently growing share commensurate with consistently growing advertising costs. But the purchase of a washing machine is a fully intelligent act—scrubbing on a ribbed board, boiling in a copper and wringing out is a long weary business. A machine which does away with it all can only be welcome, and the swift spread of ownership is hardly suprising. These authors' praise

---

* John Coulson in *On Knowing the Consumer*, Joseph W. Newman, ed., John Wiley and Sons Inc., 1966, pp. 116 ff.

† Ralph Harris and Arthur Seldon, *Advertising in Action*, Institute of Economic Affairs and Hutchinson, 1962.

for the contribution of advertising 'to a reduction in costs by enlarging the market and output' is incantation. The same applies to the increase in Harvey's wine advertising from £25,000 in 1955 to a quarter of a million pounds in 1961 which went along with a rise in demand per year of up to 40 per cent according to the type of drink. The increase must have many causal explanations. Or again, consider the rise in numbers drinking instant coffee, amongst whom the best-known and most advertised brands—Nescafé and Maxwell House—dominate the ground. In this case the sufficient and more telling explanation is the economic one we advanced in Chapter Two: the giants will always carve things up between them.

We find ourselves again faced with the fascinations and difficulties of charting not short-run and one-to-one effects but the whole movement of society registered in its popular art, in the styles and manners which reveal its values and morality, in the contradictions and tensions of its main institutions, most of all in the language of its art. But in the end, however necessary it is to keep open our scepticism about the effects of advertising, it becomes absurd to chop over the alleged findings and dispute the grounds of what we do not know and cannot prove. The power of advertising is obvious and immense. It is a main voice in our culture and what it says is very largely malignant. It speaks with the strength and authority given by its masters, men who sit in the corporate seats of power in industrial society. The dissenter has to find his voice for himself.

SIX

A Note for Dissenters

Finding a voice is a matter of finding something to talk about. Before we can discuss a part of our experience we must be able to name it. There is no doubt that a great deal of our culture, the validity and permanence of its tradition, has lapsed. A culture is a map of experience upon which a man may find his bearings and make some meanings for himself. No man stands culturally naked: he discovers where he is by reading the terrific complexity of the signals which his culture gives out, by sorting and selecting amongst them, and then by making some of them his own. In the thick-textured communities of the past, largely isolated from the rest of the country, the process was easier.* There was a rich, concrete language available which carried the essential morality of the society in heavily charged saws, proverbs, phrases and single words. Within settled limits, the individual found a vivid set of explanations, both moral and metaphysical, which permitted him a rare combination of assurance and growth. No doubt the growth he attained was the result of his own talents and efforts, but the existing language gave him a means to name, cherish and realize these. Without such words and rhythms, without rituals and actions, a man has no way of sorting and defining his experience. The antique language the peasant learned has largely gone, in Britain at least. What remains is a jumble of more or less inadequate images. The

* The historical lines of these cultures now emerge pretty clearly from an astonishing variety of researches, e.g. E. P. Thompson, *The Making of the English Working Class*, Gollancz, 1963; P. Laslett, *The World We Have Lost*, Methuen, 1965; G. E. Evans, *The Pattern Under the Plough*, Faber, 1956; W. G. Hoskins, *The Midland Peasant*, Macmillan, 1957; Joan Thirsk, *The Agrarian History of England and Wales: Vol. IV 1500–1640*, Cambridge, 1967; Joel Halpern, *Economy and Society of Laos*, Yale, 1964; Oscar Lewis, *Life in a Mexican Village*, Illinois, 1951.

most universal of these are the images of the mass media. These images issue from a system whose driving force is surplus capital. When all is said and done about the unkillable continuities of human living, about the robust toughness of the small family and its ways of living, about the vitality of dozens of minor cultural activities from gardening to madrigal groups, about the wholesome innovations made possible by chainstores and supermarkets, after these necessary acknowledgements, it remains true that the main agents of mass communications are commercial, and that they are the central source of a universal social imagery. To a significant extent they provide the map of the culture upon which men and women can find out themselves and their place. In these circumstances, then, we shall have to look very hard at the map they offer. It won't do to call out rude names from across the wall, and to offer in any simple way the road to salvation as lying through the classroom. For clearly, as I have said repeatedly, we need to know about new and old commodities and we need a system of mass communications for this and all other sorts of information. The radical correction that is called for is to convert the present state of affairs into a public and accessible system, freed of private control, open to many voices (including commercial ones). But nobody is going to make this correction for a long time yet. We shall have to do the best we can with the instruments and institutions we have to hand, and of these, as I have also said, the biggest is the educational system. It therefore follows that in a society which estimates influence by numbers education is the only institution which can exert any leverage on mass communications in general, and its commercialism in particular. There are a variety of suggestions to make.

The first is to set out the kinds of work which a dissenter might pursue. He might begin by turning up the prewar Frankfurt school of sociologists which coincided with the English work based in Cambridge as the first conscious decision to see and understand the workings of mass industrial culture. Set side by side the sixth form textbook *Culture and Environment*,* Q. D. Leavis's study of bestsellers, *Fiction and the Reading Public*,* and some of the essays on popular music and art forms in Theodore Adorno's *Prisms** or Leo Lowenthal's *Literature and the Image of Man** and *American Social Patterns*.* This last study will do for our purposes. Lowenthal shows that the heroes of

* F. R. Leavis and Denys Thompson, Chatto, 1932; Q. D. Leavis, Chatto and Windus, 1932; Adorno, now reissued by Spearman, 1970; Lowenthal, Boston, 1960.

pulp magazines in the U.S.A. during the early part of the century were what he calls 'production' heroes—the titans of industry and the robber barons such as Dreiser shows us in *The Titan* or Frank Norris shows us in the railway boss of *The Octopus*. Henry Ford, H. C. Frick, William Randolph Hearst, Samuel Insull were the progenitors of the line. By the thirties and later, the heroes had become 'consumption' figures—the celebrities of Hollywood and the metropolitan '400', the glittering playgirls of Fitzgerald's *The Great Gatsby* and Hemingway's *The Sun Also Rises*. This work gives us the tip. What are the prevailing types now, in TV and pulp fiction, and what are their relations with advertising imagery? How do we trace out and account for the peculiar ubiquity of the James Bond mythology which not only has been the success it has in films, strip cartoons and paperbacks, but has even impregnated toyshops and men's underwear with its grisly offspring. We might ask, what degree of manipulation is really there in the extravagant fantasies of *The Troubleshooters* or *The Avengers*, and to what extent do these programmes really carry the values and aspirations of their audience? We might go on to see the links of the thriller programmes with ostensibly respectable programmes like *The Forsyte Saga*. In each case, the main point of the inquiry would be to take stock of the presence of the commercial world and its symbolism in the most widely shared system of communication in history. The possibilities are limitless. These areas of the cultural map are bare. Such studies are accessible both to the academic researcher working by himself or with a few students in a university, or to a schoolteacher with a halfterm programme for bloodyminded school-leavers or eager and responsive eleven-year-olds. The university seminar would be dishonouring no clerisy if it drew in the lines of today's 'consumption' heroes in pulp fiction, and women's magazines, on TV and in advertisements; the third form would be very busy and, in many teachers' experience, very interested in doing the same thing with its own comics and magazines; the extra-mural class might do either. A sixth-form could compare the prestige and 'image-building' advertisements for Concorde over the past few years with such of the economic facts as they can discover; they could do the same for the I.C.I. 'Pathfinder' type of series or General Motors in the U.S.A. A teacher's part-time certificate course could complete its psychology requirements by taking up the whole question of the effects of advertising, and attempt some experiments to test these in schools. The sociology class at any level could study the structural connections between industry and mass communications and find out the men who wield power in both. The eleven-year-olds could turn their tireless gusto to the topics and styles of TV commercials. Their ear for cant is more than sharp enough to pick up the rich heaps of nonsense left lying about the natural breaks.

In each inquiry there must be more than a vaguely iconoclastic sense of direction. Take, for example, a detailed inquiry into the making of fashions in clothes (a very necessary piece of work). This would obviously hope to weigh up the extent to which the movement of fashion is manipulated by the manufacturers for their own profit as against the rate at which clothes wear out or are used for special purposes (e.g. work not leisure). But there could be no simple formula for analysis. Some clothes (e.g. the mini-skirt) owe a large part of their popularity to their convenience (easy to make, to wash, cool to wear) and another part to their being a sometimes defiant signal about the wearer's loyalties, values, age. The contribution made through fashion to wholly defensible standards of gaiety, prettiness, thrift, durability (all selling points in the advertisements) can't be set aside by hunting down all advertisers as witches and demons. In the same inquiry the presence of the chainstores, especially Marks and Spencers, who do not advertise but who have led strongly against the class bias and cultural hierarchies of *haute couture*, would count for a lot. There are queer obstructions in the way of a full and intelligent reading of social phenomena. Nobody would find it odd to pursue the economic factors which make a new trend in fashion, but the traditional sanctions which hedge about music make it indelicate for anyone to pursue in proper detail the covert and the barefaced manipulations which go into the manufacture of a golden disc or a Eurovision song star. *Rolling Stone* is no doubt a stylesetter and mainline rock textbook, but it is also a part of the concrete conditions of production which create an exceptionally profitable business structure, and not to see this is to convict oneself of sentimentality. Once again, the problem is to weigh up the amounts of manipulation and of free response in any part of a culture and try to ascribe responsibility. The need for rare delicacy and sureness in finding this balance comes out if we watch how a 'style' is created in the whole interaction of advertising, entertainments, and the visual arts—including, of course, film-making.* A com-

---

* Cf. the very interesting comparison in *The Popular Arts*, p. 276.

parison of *Vogue* and *Honey* models with the queens of pop and spy movies with, in turn, the bright young things of the girlie magazines would fetch up in front of the genial pluralism of the pop art painting whose artist takes his metaphors from just this world, who sees no contradictions in doing so, and who can speak unaffectedly in the accents of planned obsolescence—'they are 18 months behind New York in the Washington studios'.* To accuse the artist or the film director of complicity in the distortions of bad art and advertising is then to declare oneself a backward-looking old fuddy-duddy. But the accusation would base itself on the inquiries we have suggested, and once they are completed in the right density and specific gravity, the evaluations follow unanswerably. At the moment art in our society regularly hires itself out to its commercial masters. Individuals who might feel bitterly at odds with this state of affairs can share no community of values and, more urgently, can find nowhere else to earn their wages. This will change only if large areas of social relations and conditions of production change. At the moment the romantic ethic of the lonely artist endorses the commercial ethic of the individual consumer. We need a more generous and shared conception of art.

These drastic changes are always possible, but only according to the lines of existing or of latent institutions. The most powerful institution to hand for these purposes is, as we can all see, the educational system. It can start out at all levels with the sort of inquiry I sketch out. Nor is that inquiry only beginning now. I have mentioned the pioneers of such social research both in this country and in Europe, and long before the thirties Britain had known a succession of criticisms of and resistance to the degrading aspects of industrial capitalism. The voices of William Morris, Ruskin, Carlyle and Matthew Arnold are still audible. Today the extensive work in secondary schools, polytechnic courses and colleges of education on the peculiarities of advertising is evidence that dissent is no innovation. The lack is, first, of real collaboration and, second, of a coherent critique within which to define and understand local objections. Without a consistent theory about the significance of advertising in society small scale analyses get lost. This is what tends to happen in schools, so while a sixteen-year-old can see quite clearly that the girl in the ad won't always look good enough to eat, the single objection has no weight in a universe of such girls. The available structure of feeling and ideas is stronger than the objection.

* Quoted by Randall Jarrell, 'Sad Heart at the Supermarket', *Daedalus*, Spring 1960.

Resistance must be systematic. This book aims to provide a systematic critique which makes sense and shape out of dozens of individual and rightly sardonic objections to advertising.

Let us stress again that this critique does not have only educational point. There is and has been for a long time a good deal of social and political action in concert against advertising. There has been explicit legislation: The Town and Country Planning Act of 1947* together with the later additions to its terms was a conscious reaction to the invasion of a people's landscape by commercial forces. A main provision was against defacing scenery by advertising. Like the legislation brought in to forbid cigarette advertising on television (1966), to say nothing of the television advertising levy, the Act caused a brief quarrel over the freedom of the individual which was allegedly inhibited by these controls. But the point is narrowly individualist. A garage owner now cannot display more than a limited amount of forecourt advertising. Which freedom counts for more? The petrol companies who would invade the town and particularly the countryside with a chaos of baleful signs, or the people who come to find a stretch of countryside which is not blown open by ugliness and would live in towns less hemmed in by instructions to spend? In a sane society there would be no argument. In a civilized society the rejoinder to the critics of advertising that 'advertisements cheer the place up' would be as redundant as it is now pitiful confession that in our public efforts, our efforts at collective action, we can only make a seedy and grubby environment which breeds the magic fantasies of advertising as the only available form of escape. Yet in single attacks on advertising there are real gains to be marked up. The efforts of the now defunct Consumer Advisory Council† in their various pamphlets and the Consumers' Association in *Which?*† (the association also publishes *The Good Food Guide*) have led to a very much more widespread knowledge about value for money in individual purchases. Their continued stamina has probably done more than any other group to carry through the 1968 Trade Descriptions Act which makes untrue statements about goods illegal, clarifies the definition of key words used about goods and services, and requires traders to give information about their wares.

* Town and Country Planning Act 1947, Section 31 and 32 and (same act) Control of Advertisements Regulations 1960 (S.I. 1960, no. 695) and 1969. Cf. *Hansard*, 11 December 1969.

† 14 Buckingham St, W.C.2.

The Consumers' Association has thrived. The Advertising Inquiry Council has faltered, died, and just to say revived again. But what is needed is for individual bodies to push to the back of their individual enterprises and see what connections can be established in the territory beyond. It is not in the least utopian to think of local consumer councils, with ready access to local radio stations, not only watching and reporting on all kinds of local services from dentists to supermarkets, but also carrying through a national programme of reports and debates. The hero for such plans must of course be Ralph Nader. Individual campaigns like the anti-Concorde or third airport protests or the Civic Trust need to link up with apparently unrelated organizations like *Shelter* or *Oxfam* (both exceptionally large examples of voluntary institutions) in order to find out how alike their intentions are in circulating information which contradicts or reverses the flow of official information. Each of these bodies in one or another way wishes to affect public opinion and to alter the movement and nature of official information. As long as they continue to work in isolation they are—in a society which weighs influence by numbers—less effective. In this proposed confederation the independent bodies with government backing, like the Council of Industrial Design, would need strengthening. It would then be perfectly possible for educational centres with access to research funds—such as the Schools Council or Nuffield—to join hands across many dimensions with the welfare and amenity organizations in an effort to provide a larger, more disinterested, more human and dignified version of society than is easy to find today.

These efforts, which would organize and give reality to the feelings and hopes of a great many people in society, would precede a long and difficult programme of public legislation. Such a programme would include a thoroughgoing increase in the publication of details of new legislation. There is crying need, for example, for public information about the Race Relations Act, the changeover to comprehensive schools, about land conservation and about welfare and unemployment benefits. Very few people understand any of the arguments. The arguments are not impenetrable. No government has tried to educate the people about its most important actions. Responsible and democratic government would begin in education. It might go on to fix much tougher limits to the sums allowed to the corporations as tax-free advertising expenditure, and at the same time scrutinize the profits on monopolies and retail price-fixing much more closely. Finally, the future government might provide funds to the independent institutions (and the BBC) for research into the workings of mass communications and for the better broadcasting of necessary debate, knowledge, and reason.

These proposals sound insanely hopeful in the present state of affairs. For a long time, the BBC has been, in its arbitrary way, a live and growing hope that a national communication system may one day speak for a nation. The partial nature of its governing body always made it liable to wilfulness and malice. Such malice is available in large measures. It is likely that for some years air, time and radio waves will be sold off to nameless cheque books for the sake of a quick quid. The control over information, public and unobstructed argument, and the diffusion of a free and equal culture will be—in the interests of cash—tighter than ever before.

There are one or two cracks in the surface. In 1971, so far as I know for the first time in Britain, the terms of an industrial dispute were set out by the management and union involved. The Post Office and the Union of Post Office Workers each took advertisement space in national newspapers to argue its case. Since the power of international capital over labour has worked so strongly in a general climate of ignorance and mean-minded chauvinism to misrepresent organized labour claims, especially on the mass media, this attempt to begin public education cuts sharply against the usual flow of information. The second crack is in a very different area. But there are grounds for hope when so stolid and unimaginative a body as the British Medical Association can press for a campaign of public advertising and information to check and, finally eliminate smoking as a fatal addiction. I have discussed cigarette advertisement above. Since the first BMA report on smoking in 1962 there has been a sporadic and weak-kneed attempt to advertise against the addiction. But the energy of the campaign after the 1971 report is much more concentrated and the statistics more final and unanswerable. For once in a way, the weight of a minority (as they say) may move successfully against the interests of the juggernauts. Every man lives as a member of many minorities: housing (*Shelter*), world poverty (*Oxfam, Action for World Development*) derelict children (*Child Poverty Action Group*), smoking (*BMA*), landscape (*Civic Trust*), wage claims and inflation (*TUC*)—there is a satisfactory explanation to relate these concerns and these groups within one frame. They all command a wide segment of public feeling and support. It is their function to make the connections; to counter the flow of information from the centres of power; to release into circulation contradictory knowledge; to generate the resistance, the fight which must be set up whenever rational debate begins.

For in the end, of course, there is no substitute for reason and debate.

What is it to be rational? It is a necessary condition of rationality that a man shall formulate his beliefs in such a way that it is clear what evidence would be evidence *against* them and that he shall lay himself open to criticism and refutation in the light of any possible objection. But to foreclose on tolerance is precisely to cut oneself off from such criticism and refutation. It is to gravely endanger one's own rationality by not admitting one's own fallibility.

One of the most urgent of contemporary tasks is to insist on subjecting the social and political order to continuous rational criticism and to preserve the autonomy of rational enquiry in universities and elsewhere. The institutionalization of rationality was one of the great achievements of bourgeois society. Of course the very fact of institutionalization can be used to try to isolate the practice of rational criticism and so prevent it being exercised upon the social order ... assaults upon rational enquiry in the interests of the established social order have to be resisted.

The organization of rational argument and the maintenance of such criticism against the attempts to isolate it by those hardheaded men who would call the critics 'idealists', 'unrealists', 'utopians', has been the main task of this book.

One cannot liberate people from above; one cannot re-educate them at this fundamental level. As the young Marx saw, men must liberate themselves, The only education that liberates is self-education. To make men objects of liberation by others is to assist in making them passive instruments, is to cast them for the role of inert matter to be moulded into forms chosen by the élite. The majority of men in advanced industrial societies are often confused, unhappy and conscious of their lack of power; they are often also hopeful. critical and able to grasp immediate possibilities of happiness and freedom.★

These possibilities recede and diminish day by day. Advertising, the voice of the groups of men who would run civilization to their own ends, tries consistently to refashion happiness and freedom until they may be bought for cash across the counters of department stores. At the same time, if its members would only take their chances, the power of the educational institutions has grown well beyond the point at which they could break this system open. There is nothing inevitable about victory for either side.

★ Alasdair MacIntyre, *Marcuse*, Fontana (Modern Masters), 1970, pp. 91-2.

APPENDIX

A Defence of Thorn Lighting (see pp. 98–9)

If one can't illustrate a factory worker when selling a product designed for the factory, whom may one show? Or does the crime lie in illustrating him *well*? Or in attempting to sell factory lighting at all?

Difficult questions, and Mr Inglis's commentary isn't helpful. In one breath he describes the picture as 'realistic' (Sweaty vest, grimy cheek, etc.). In the next, he claims that it romanticizes working conditions, putting smell and dirt 'at a distance' beneath a high gloss. A critic's critic might say that he was making ex post facto rationalizations of a preconceived thesis, and twisting them to suit his text at that.

The advertisement is designed to sell Atlas Lighting, but the suggestion that it demeans the worker shown, by calling 'this man's life' into service, is well below the belt. He isn't being placed in thrall, nor crucified on capital's cross of gold: he is standing in front of a camera for a few hours. And the product is intended to profit him, as well as Atlas, by improving his working conditions.

Acknowledgements

The author and publisher wish to thank the following for permission to reprint copyright material: Arthur Miller for the extract from *Death of a Salesman* Copyright © 1955 by Arthur Miller, from *Collected Plays*, Secker & Warburg Ltd; Macmillan & Co. Ltd for three extracts from *The General Theory of Employment, Interest and Money* by J. M. Keynes; W. G. Runciman and Routledge & Kegan Paul Ltd for extract from *Relative Deprivation and Social Justice*; Francis Harmar Brown for the article 'Not so much a defence of Advertising as an attack on its critics' from *The Times*, 14 May 1970; Penguin Books Ltd for extract from *A Fortunate Man* by John Berger and Jean Mohr, copyright © John Berger and Jean Mohr, 1967, 1969; Oxford University Press for extract from *Power Elite* by C. Wright Mills; Her Majesty's Stationery Office for extract from N.B.P.I. Report No. 141. *Costs and Revenue of National Newspapers*, Cmnd. 4277.

The plates are reproduced by kind permission of the following:

Plates 1 and 2: Vanguard Press Inc. from pp. 79 and 85 of *The Mechanical Bride* by Marshall McLuhan

Plate 3: Bamforth & Co Ltd from Card No. 2449

Plate 4: Kellogg's and J. Walter Thompson Ltd

Plate 5: British Leyland (Austin–Morris) Ltd and Dorland Advertising Ltd

Plate 6: Gallaher Ltd and Collett Dickenson Pearce and Partners Ltd

Plate 7: Barclays Bank Ltd and Charles Barker Advertising Ltd

Plate 8: British Steel Corporation and Ogilvy Benson and Mather Ltd

Plate 9: Mary Quant Cosmetics Ltd and Aalders, Marchant, Weinreich Ltd

Plate 10: Courtaulds Ltd and Ogilvy Benson and Mather Ltd

Plate 11: Thorn Lighting Ltd and Ogilvy Benson and Mathers Ltd

Plate 12: Times Newspapers Ltd

The advertising rates in Chapter Two are reproduced by permission of the newspapers and television companies concerned. Other tables in Chapter Two are acknowledged in the note stating the source at the foot of each table.

Bibliography

Critiques and Diagnosis

Adler-Karlsson, G., *Western Economic Warfare 1947–67*, Stockholm 1968.

Baker, S. S., *The Permissible Lie*, Peter Owen 1969.

Barratt Brown, M., *After Imperialism*, rev. edn, Merlin Press 1969.

——, 'Economics and Advertising', unpublished paper.

Berger, J., *A Fortunate Man*, Allen Lane, The Penguin Press 1967.

Birch, L., *The Advertising We Deserve*, Vista Books 1962.

Boorstin, J., *The Image*, Weidenfeld & Nicholson 1962.

Brown, J. A. C., *Techniques of Persuasion from Propaganda to Brainwashing*, Penguin 1963.

Clairemonte, F., *Economic Liberalism and Under-development*, Bombay, Asia Publishing House 1960.

Gervasi, S., 'A Structural Analysis of Mass Communications', unpublished paper.

Cmnd. 1753, *Report of the Committee on Broadcasting*, HMSO 1962.

Glyn, A. and Sutcliffe B., 'The Critical Condition of British Capital', *New Left Review 66*, 1971.

Hall, S., 'Class and the Mass Media', *Class*, R. Mabey ed., Blond 1961.

Hall, S. and Whannel, P., *The Popular Arts*, Hutchinson 1964.

Henry, J., *Culture Against Man*, Tavistock 1966.

Hobsbawm, E., *Industry and Empire*, Weidenfeld & Nicolson 1967.

Hoggart, R., *The Uses of Literacy*, Chatto & Windus 1958.

Holbrook, D., *The Secret Places*, Methuen 1963.

Jonson, B., *The Alchemist*, London 1612.

Kaldor, N. H., 'The Economic Aspects of Advertising', *Review of Economic Studies 45*, 1950–51.

Kaldor, N. H. and Silverman, R., *Advertising Expenditure and Revenue of the Press*, Cambridge, 1948.

Kelley, S., *Professional Public Relations and Political Power*, Johns Hopkins 1956.

Leavis, F. R. and Thompson, D., *Culture and Environment*, Chatto & Windus 1933.

Little, I. M. and Reyner, A. C., *Higgledy-Piggledy Growth Again*, Kelley, New York 1968.

Marcuse, H., *One-Dimensional Man*, Boston 1964.

MacIntyre, A. C., 'The Strange Death of Social Democratic England', *Listener*, 4 July 1968.

——, *Against the Self-Images of the Age*, Duckworth 1971.

McGuinness, J., *The Selling of the President*, André Deutsch 1970.

McLuhan, H. M., *The Mechanical Bride: Folklore of Modern Industrial Man*, Vanguard, New York 1951.

134

Bibliography

Melman, S., *Pentagon Capitalism: The Political Economy of War*, McGraw-Hill 1970.
Mills, C. Wright, *White Collar*, Oxford 1955.
——, *The Sociological Imagination*, Oxford 1959.
——, *The Power Elite*, Oxford and New York 1956.
Nader, R., 'A Consummer's Guide to the Economy', *New York Review of Books*, September 4, 1971.
Packard, V., *The Hidden Persuaders*, Penguin 1966.
Report of the Reith Commission on Advertising, Labour Party 1969.
Rosenberg, B. and White, D. M., eds, *Mass Culture The Popular Arts in America*, Free Press, Glencoe U.S.A. 1957.
Runciman, W. G., *Relative Deprivation and Social Justice*, Routledge 1966.
Scanlon, H., 'International Combines versus the Unions', *Bulletin of the Institute for Workers Control*, 1, 4, 1969.
Tawney, R. H., *The Acquisitive Society*, Bell 1921.
Thompson, D., *Voice of Civilization*, Muller 1943.
Thompson, E. P., ed., *Warwick University Ltd*, Penguin 1970.
Todd, J., *The Big Sell*, Lawrence & Wishart 1961.
Turner, D., *Semi-Detached*, Methuen 1962.
Tunstall, J., *The Advertising Man*, Chapman & Hall 1964.
Whitehead, F. S., 'Advertising' in *Discrimination and Popular Culture*, D. Thompson ed., rev. edition Penguin 1972.
Williams, R., *Communications*, Penguin 1962.
——, 'Crisis in Communications', *Listener* 31 July 1969.
——, 'The Magic System', *New Left Review 4*, 1960.
——, ed., *May Day Manifesto*, Penguin 1968.

Methods and Statistics

Adorno, T. W., *Prisms*, Spearman (reissued) 1970.
Advertising Directory, Institute of Practitioners of Advertising.
Austin, J. L., *How to do Things With Words*, J. O. Urmston ed., Oxford 1962.
BBC Handbook (annually).
Campaign, Haymarket Press, London W2.
Goffman, E., *Presentation of Self in Everyday Life*, Doubleday, New York 1959.
Halloran, J. D., *The Effects of Mass Communication*, Leicester University Press 1965.
——, *Attitude Formation and Change*, New York, Humanities Press 1965.
——, ed., *The Effects of Television*, Panther 1970.
Himmelweit, H., Oppenheim, A. N., and Vince, P., *Television and the Child*, Oxford 1958.
ITV Handbook (annually).
Keynes, J. M., *The General Theory of Employment, Interest and Money*, Macmillan 1936.
Klapper, J. T., *The Effects of Mass Communications*, Glencoe Free Press 1961.
Krugman, H., The Impact of TV Advertising, *Public Opinion Quarterly* XXXIX, 3, 1965.
Lowenthal, L., *American Social Patterns*, Boston 1957.
Lazarsfeld, P., *The People's Choice*, Columbia New York 1948.

Lyle, J., Schramm, W. and Parker, A., *Television in the Lives of Our Children*, Oxford New York 1961.

MacIntyre, A. C., 'A Mistake About Causality in Social Science' in P. Laslett and W. G. Runciman, eds, *Politics, Philosophy and Society*, 2nd series, Blackwell 1962.

Market Research, Haymarket Press, London W.C.2.

Market Research Society, *Research in Advertising* 1963.

National Board for Prices and Incomes, *Costs and Revenue of National Newspapers*, HMSO 1970.

Seibert, J. and Wills, G., eds, *Marketing Research*, Penguin 1971.

Taylor, C., *The Explanation of Behaviour*, Routledge 1965.

Apologetics and Businessmen's Primers

Aharoni, Y., 'How to Market a Country', *Columbia Journal of World Business*, Spring 1966.

Backman, J., *Advertising and Competition*, New York University Press 1967.

Bernays, E. L., *The Engineering of Consent*, University of Oklahoma Press 1955.

Black, S., *Practical Public Relations*, Pitman 1962.

Britt, S. H., *Consumer Behaviour and the Behavioural Sciences*, John Wiley, New York 1967.

Cadman, M. H., *Business Economics*, Macmillan 1969.

Charvat, F. J., *Supermarketing*, Macmillan, New York 1961.

Child, J., *British Management Thought*, Allen & Unwin 1969.

Colley, R. H., *Defining Advertising Goals*, New York, Association of National Advertisers 1961.

Crane, E., *Marketing Communications—A Behavioural Approach to Men, Marketing and Media*, John Wiley, New York 1967.

Davies, A. H. and Palmer, O. W., *Market Research and Scientific Distribution*, Blandford Press 1957.

Dichter, E., *The Strategy of Desire*, Boardman 1960.

——, 'The World Customer', in *Harvard Business Review*, July–August 1962.

Ehrenberg, A. S. C. and Pyatt, S. G., eds, *Consumer Behaviour*, Penguin 1970.

Faville, D. E., *Selected Cases of Marketing Management*, Prentice Hall 1961.

Glasser, R., *The New High Priesthood: the social, ethical and political implications of a marketing orientated society*, Macmillan 1967.

——, *Planned Marketing*, Business Publications 1964.

Greyser, S. A., 'Businessmen Re Advertising', *Harvard Business Review*, May–June 1962.

Harris, R. and Seldon, A., *Advertising in a Free Society*, Institute of Economic Affairs, 1959.

——, *Advertising in Action*, Institute of Economic Affairs 1962.

Kotler, P., *Marketing Management: Analysis, Planning and Control*, Prentice-Hall 1967.

Lowndes, D., *Marketing: The Uses of Advertising*, Pergamon 1971.

Meyerhoff, A. E., *The Strategy of Persuasion: The Use of Advertising Skills in Fighting the Cold War*, New York, Berkeley Publishing Corporation 1968

Reeves, R., *Reality in Advertising*, Knoff, New York 1961.

Simon, J., *Management Advertising*, Prentice Hall International 1971.
Swindells, A. P. F., *Advertising Media and Campaign Planning*, Butterworths 1966.
Taplin, W., *The Origin of Television Advertising in the United Kingdom*, Pitman 1961.
Thompson, H. Underwood., *Product Strategy*, Business Publications 1962.
Turner, E. S., *The Shocking History of Advertising*, Michael Joseph 1952.
Utley, T. E., *Enoch Powell, The Man and His Thinking*, London 1968.
Wingo, W., *Pattern for Success*, Tadworth 1969.

List of Tables (pp. 19–31)

Index